Is 'Black' Really Beautiful?

Dehumanizing and Intentional Ethics of Descriptions and Vilifying Philosophies of Naming

Kuir ë Garang

The Nile Press
Calgary, Alberta

Copyright © 2013 by KUIR ë GARANG

All rights reserved. No part of this book may be reproduced or transmitted in any form or by any means, electronic, mechanical, photocopying or recording, without written permission of The Nile Press.

For reproduction of any section of the book for scholarly or literary purposes, write to The Nile Press.

First Edition 2013

ISBN: 978-0-9916789-4-5

PUBLISHED BY THE NILE PRESS
http://thenilepress.com
Calgary
Printed in Canada

But negroes, like other people, act upon motives. Why should they do any thing for us, if we will do nothing for them? If they stake their lives for us, they must be prompted by the strongest motive——even the promise of freedom. And the promise being made, must be kept.

(US President, Abraham Lincoln (letter to James C. Conkling dated August 26, 1863)

FOR MONICA

You are deligent and industrious. That's an admirable quality. Keep it up!

APRIL 17, 2013

Calgary, AB

TABLE OF CONTENTS

PREFACE.. vii

CHAPTER ONE
Sense of Self Color-Wise...1
   1.1 Self as a Defined Entity (Ontic Significance)..........2
   1.2 The Colored American..5
   1.3 The Colored African...17

CHAPTER TWO
Blackness and Whiteness Ontically Speaking...............29
   2.1 Historical Backdrop..30
   2.2 Blackness..34
   2.3 The People and their Color 42
   2.4 Whiteness 52

CHAPTER THREE
Racism^R verses Racism^r: Reality and Social Construction of Race......63
   3.1 Race as an empirical reality.................................64
   3.2 Misuse of Science 68
   3.3 Fear and Racial Instability...................................72

CHAPTER FOUR
Contemporary Racism^R (Racehood):
A Product of Mentally Disturbed................................75
   4.1 Racism Defined...76
   4.2 Racism Instrumentalized.....................................80

CHAPTER FIVE
The 'Nigger' Word: Illusion and Truth..........................91
   5.1 Diminution of History a s a Point of View 92
   5.2 Necessity of Burying the 'N' word 94
   5.3 Illusion of Avoiding the 'N' word 96

CHAPTER SIX
The Excusable..103
   6.1 Thoughts Authentication 103
   6.2 The 'Unmonkey' Business................................109

    6.3 The 'Unmonkeyness' of the Colored Africanness 110

CHAPTER SEVEN
    Summary and Conclusion..113
APPENDIX...117
NOTES..121
BIBILIOGRAPHY.. 133
INDEX...139

PREFACE

This book was inspired by three situations: my life and work in culturally and racially diverse environments and *situations*, my work with immigrants of all Races and works of life, and more so, how 'people of color' are described and how they view themselves. What I came to realize through these colorful experiences is that many assumptions people make about others are misguided and, at times, *innocent*. While a good number of us connive at the assumptions we make about others, many among us are true with our feelings. However, we don't always realize and acknowledge the dangers these innocent feelings engender. When people are subjected to what Chimamanda Adichie calls '*The Danger of a Single Story*,' what one has to consider are the intentions of those making the *assumptions*. Some of those assumers are true to their feelings and have no ill-feelings regarding the assumptions they make. Their assumptions, in this case, are pure, innocent exposure to a *one-sided story*. These assumers are not always aware of how emotionally paralyzing and practically oppressive their *innocent assumptions* are.

However, I've come to realize also that we all change with time. While changes that come to us are, at first, regarded with utmost caution, the value of change, at times, transcends our fears and we soon find ourselves embracing the very ideas we'd previously regarded with hesitation if not disdain. Necessity sometimes makes abhorred things objects of desire. However much one wants to stick to the old methods with every might of the *will*, necessity pushes or pulls one toward equilibrating conditions (whatever they are).

In our contemporary times, we all need jobs (or some form of income) to support our families. We need our kids to go to school and be fair-minded members of the society they live in. We also need friends and neighbors who respect our feelings. These are *absolute* universalities. However, an arrogant and ill-informed heart might be blinded by excessive pride not to see the fact that every man or woman we see on the streets *thinks* about his or her family's well-being. Every child we see hopes to grow up and be helpful (even if some don't) to *the* parents who'd been instrumental in her upbringing. What remains puzzling is that the preceding claims are acknowledged to be truly authentic, but people still act contrary to these accepted claims. We still look down on others. We still take advantage of weak people if a given situation warrants. We still act in our own interest but justify our actions by claiming benefits to the people we hurt in the process of satisfying our insatiable interests. This is manifested by US invasion of Iraq and Afghanistan and the March 2011 NATO airstrike against Libya disguised as 'protection of civilians.'

While simple *human nature* is to blame for all the misgivings we breathe every single day, one has to remember the unequivocal evolutionary steps we've taken away from nature's compound complexity and individual self-interest. It is uncontroversial to say that self-interest is our pronounced natural proclivity. Still, evolutionary gravity resists such a tendency.

Desire to temper with powerful people's natural proclivities is regarded naïve and impractical solution-wise. This shouldn't be the case. The proclivities of these supposedly *untouchables* should be braved because unethical and derogatory description of people has long-term detrimental effects on people. Factors such as deliberate suppressions of the truth about *a* people's history are contributing factors to such unethical descriptions. And George James, in his ground-breaking book, *Stolen Legacy*, puts it beautifully that for people of all colors to understand themselves, there has to be 'a proper appraisal of each other.'[1] But can one come up with a status quo that smells of inclusivity? I know one virtue that can allow us to think inclusively of others: HUMILITY; a virtue that is hard to accept, but necessary for noble inclusivity.

As an immigrant settlement worker, I've helped many families from different Races and cultures. The families have one thing in common: *seeking the best living standards for their families*. As much as nature deterministically dictates some of our actions, transcending some of the nature's destructive effects can be achieved through multiplications of *humble selves*. How, you may ask? This is possible simply through unassuming, ungrudging acceptance of our natural, embarrassing weaknesses: the fount of undesired but necessary salvational selves.

My aim in this book is to challenge (not eliminate) destructive status quos and the almost deified unethical descriptions of people. Traditional Racism^R in all its forms and manifestations is despicable. Note that racism (Racism^r), not Racism^R, isn't necessarily bad. But we have to understand first what Racism¹ and racism mean for any differentiation to make any sense.

I therefore intend to equalize humanity by exegetically reducing racism to inner, proud feelings about one's Race, whatever these feelings may be. We are all composed of feelings of self at different times. How good or bad such feelings of self are depends on circumstances of our times, and how our intellect conceptualizes them in relation to how we want others to perceive us. Simply put, the aim of the book is to drum home the thought that *all people are equal only that our perception of them is different given our social, political and religious indoctrinations; indoctrinations that lead to unethical racial descriptions.*

For starters, I used the word 'colorless' for people of European descent to make talks of 'colored people' sensible; and to also make sure Africans and people of African descent are cut some historical, fairness slack. The words 'white' and 'black' are in question (only in this work) and have not been used in exegetical texts unless a given situation requires. Still, as a matter of prudential requirement and racial sensitivities, I must note that while the word 'colorless' might offend some people (of unconscionable and conscionable integrities), I make no apologies for its use because it is meant to bring to the fore why the value of ethical description of *a* human population and equality of people should be considered with moral priority. Any conscientious colorless person will understand where I'm coming from; even with a tinge of historical taste. The word colorless also makes sense of the word 'colored' in our daily usage of 'colored'. The book needs absolute humility and ungrudging *sense of self* when reading. This is a test of one's emotive elasticity: colored and colorless people alike.

---

¹ Racism^R and racism^r will be delineated and explained in Chapter Four.

Δ

Chapter One deals with sense of self in relation to racial colors from ontic as well as conceptualization standpoint. This take includes how a person of color perceives herself to be from her own conceptualization of her own self by herself without any external procurement, and from the way she's been described by others. A conceptualization of *self* from within and without says a lot about a given person's position in any given society.

A good example of this conceptualization of self is how people of color bleach or try to change their physical appearances. Michael Jackson is one good example and Jamaican musician, Vybz Kartel another. Others include Sammy Sosa, Kofi Olimede, Mbilia Bel and Mshoza.

In **Chapter Two**, I present whiteness, blackness, their conceptuallization and their impressive owners and ownerships. The aim is to help people differentiate between the color that describes them and who they are *per se*.[2] People are, most of the time, innocently lost in the 'ontics' of their colors if not given an exegetical avenues of explicating compendium.

Chapter Three tackles the reality of Race. The argument is that race is an empirical reality that shouldn't be ignored. Its physical manifestation is something that is apparent and ignoring it only aggravates and promotes the problems race-related issues engender. It aggravates the problems because what is real is being denied; therefore, making the fight against 'Fundamentalist Racism' self-serving and escapists.

Chapter Four explains what Racism is and presents a new understanding of the reality of Racism. This new understanding maintains that racism *per se* isn't necessarily bad. What makes it bad are the circumstances surrounding it and the use to which people who have misconceived or low sense of selves put it to. For example, white supremacists who are only proud of being 'white' without using that feeling of racial self to kill or intimidate others, aren't necessarily doing anything bad. That benign, natural 'racism' (pride) is socially healthy for them and

---

[2] Maya Angelou wrote *in Graduation* that she had to 'listen to charges being brought against my color...' Color instead of Me. Color becomes *Her*. See Neuleib et al., p.43

psychologically and evolutionarily necessary. Yes, they are *racists* (like every Race) but not in the bad way we normally think they are: that is, *Racists*.

Chapter Five presents both the logic behind the disdain for the 'N' word and how silly any attempts to avoid or exterminate the 'N' word are self-serving, self-deceiving illusions. The chapter maintains that avoiding the word because of the historical anger is inadequate and leads to perpetual use of the word in a derogatory manner. Besides, targeting one 'N' word and leaving other potentially destructive descriptiveness is ineffective.

Chapter Six explains how valuable a message in any written work (scientific or otherwise) should be of some benefit to humanity. While the nature of some scholarly works can't allow this to happen, it has to be inherent in the text that such a situation (benefit to humanity) was impossible because of the nature of the work.

The Race debate of the 1920s and 1930s had supposedly scientific works that tried to prove superiority of one Race over another. A contemporary example of pointless pseudoscientific works is that of Satoshi Kanazawa of London School of economics, who believed he'd scientifically proven that black women are less attractive than women of other Races. The point of such works baffles me.

The book is therefore premised on the understanding that whatever discriminatory attitudes one has, stem from how one feels about one self and how that internal feeling is translated into relational, actional existence towards others. This understanding of sense of self is also closely tied to the required assumption that people's color and who they are *per se* are not one and the same. Both the *color* and *mere sense of self* have been grave intellectually to the 'African' person all over the world.

Method and Information

While this work has references and available literature cited, it is highly an original work that is markedly opinionated and analytical. It is not based on a broad-based research; however, the opinions presented are backed-up by available literature, everyday experiences (both mine and others') and the phenomenon of racial uneasiness in our contemporary understanding of Race relations. And above all, someone is not your friend until after reconciliation; that is, after you've annoyed them. And a meaningful Race relation is not possible if all have not been annoyed and given an opportunity to forgive.

Kuir ë Garang,
Calgary, Alberta,
January 2013

Books by Kuir ë Garang

Trifles (Novel)
Carcass Valley (Poetry)
Exegesis of Despotism (Poetry)
The Pipers and the First Phase (Novel)

CHAPTER ONE

Sense of Self Color-Wise

A**PART** from people of European descent, everyone else in the world is wary of how she looks. This is not of course on individual basis but on racial basis. We can look at Hollywood and easily find numerous examples of Euro-Americans who aren't comfortable with the way they look. And many plastic surgeons in California should thank that sentiment for making them a fortune.

However, what I am referring to is largely self-consciousness and inferiority inflections on a global, racial basis. Many Africans try to bleach and we have Michael Jackson and Vybz Kartel to thank for those examples. We also have many Chinese and Japanese who try to change the way their eyes and faces look to feel good about themselves. I am not going to cite references because one can just google such examples and be appalled. Skin-bleaching is a multimillion-dollar industry in India too.

These instances tell us that how one feels about oneself underwrites many of the things one does. Many people around the world have lost racial standards internal to them in search of euro-standards. And when it comes to color, one can easily look at Africa, Jamaica and India to see that people prefer lighter skin. What follows in this chapter is a look at how one's sense of self affects one's conceptualization of one's entire humanity relative to that of others.

1.1 Self as an Existential Entity (Ontic Significance)

How a *person* feels about himself or herself is the best *endowment* nature has imparted on each and *every* individual. I can shamelessly posit that such a postulate is exclusively true. The *objective truthfulness* of such a position (feeling about one's self) is something I'll leave open for others to ponder. Unlike Harry Frankfurt in *On Bullshit*, I do believe honesty is as hard as the pursuit of the objective truth.[1] This can easily be seen with what Obama has become as *a* president of United States.

From a man who cares about the average, poor person; to a man who kills civilians in the name of 'truth.' The monsters of the White House have monstrous, 'immolarizing' effect on 'good' people; making them unconscionably immoral and dishonest. Yes, honesty is nearer to us than objectivity, but maintaining honesty for an appreciable amount of time is hard to deal with and that makes its realization even harder or rarer than objectivity. And we know that when one says the truth, one is being *objective*. But this changes little if not nothing about how we present ourselves to others. We present an impression that we are being honest in whatever we do. There are times when how a person perceives him or herself appears contrary (such as feeling of resentment of one's own self) to any positive outlook of that given person. It would appear that such a feeling of resentment is *not* an endowment but a curse. Because there is so much bullshit in our society now[2], we tend to take the words of these confusing souls either for granted, or for what they put before us. And I disagree with Frankfurt's modesty in arguing that there is nothing in theory and experience that proves a special position that one has in relation to judgement about one's own self. There are cases in which one's judgement about one self can be rendered questionable, however, these are exceptional medical conditions. Frankfurt writes that "Facts about ourselves are not peculiarly solid and resistant to skeptical dissolution. Our natures are indeed, elusively insubstantial —notoriously less stable and less inherent than the nature of other things. And in so far as this is the case, sincerity itself is bullshit."[3] This is a designed response that is modestly relevant but practically and factually wanting.

This position is also undermined by its generality. 'Facts about ourselves' claim needs to be explained to make the claim less general. John Locke asked in *Essay Concerning Human Understanding* (Book II, chapter 1) thus: "Can another Man perceive that I am conscious of anything, when I perceive it not myself?" He added that if a person has to know something about me which I don't know, that person "must needs [sic] to have a penetrating sight, who can certainly see, that I think, when I cannot perceive it myself…" What we have to understand from Locke's assertion is not thinking *per se*, but the whole idea of knowing oneself. Even with the advances in neuroscience, what can be known about me is that I'm thinking, not what I'm thinking about. What 'I'm thinking' is a key to who I am. Purely thinking is not enough to let others know me clearly. What I think is my privilege alone. There have been new developments in Neuroscience that might put that position into question. But so far, they're only a scientific promise. A group of scientists, in Helen Wills Neuroscience Institute in University of California at Berkeley, were able to convert brain waves into 'recognizable words'. The words from the brain activity were converted to words through a computer program. The process is called *functional magnetic resonance*. Let's hope it gets out of the lab.

While some facts about ourselves are questionable when it comes to personal understanding of them, there are a lot whose insightful understanding rests solely with the possessors of the 'facts'.

We have to remember this. Manifestation of self-esteem (or mere sense of self) has a medley of manifestations in different people. Some people show it with Aristotelian and Platonic modesty and moderation.[4] Others manifest it with a remarkably shameful profundity.[5] Yet still, others disguise it with a purported sense of egalitarianism, humanitarianism and religious utilitarianism.

So, how a given person feels about himself or herself is a greater (if not the only) part of who that person is.[6] Everything, which such a person does, revolves around such a sense of self. This sense of self might be internalized or externalized. However, this sense of self is governed by a myriad of conditions. Some of these conditions are real and appreciably decent while others are flattering and misconceived. Yet still, others are real but monstrous and detestable such as the devilish inner monster of Bill Zeller. And Harry Frankfurt can't say that the monster Bill Zeller was feeling was less solid than some of the things Bill Zeller encountered in life.[7] I don't need 'science' to tell me that my sense of my *self* is concrete compared to my perception of things external to me. Frankfurt is being overly modest. This modesty has a role to play when it comes to moral impartiality though. Too much belief in one's sense of self, or facts relating to oneself, might compromise impartiality; upsetting one's moral sense. The largest part of the monstrous *otherness* is too much importance vested on the general 'I'. We will see later, in Chapter Four, how too much pride in one's Race can be destructive to oneself and others.

What is amazing, if not disappointing, is that inter-racial conditions that are decent are most of the time downplayed or made fun of. And the conditions that are flattering and misconceived are imparted with so much unspeakable potency that their evaluation becomes real and fixated beyond anybody's wild imagination. Even learned heads are driven into *unproductive negativity zone* by their porous *sense of self* to say the unfortunate yet understandable: sense-of-self-elevation and contemptible nonsense (pseudoscience). If London School of economics psychologist, Satoshi Kanazawa, suggests that 'black' women are less attractive than women of other Races, then the most sensible thing that one should do is to feel sorry for him.[8] Kanazawa's argument that presumably uses science is geared towards proving something that just beats the imagination of all intellective enterprises in terms of its purpose. When he says black men are more attractive than men of other races, then we know science, like religious books, is being used for a desired end. We'll see more of these vanities in the following chapters.

1.2 The Colored American

From 'discovery' of Africa, to slavery and colonization of Africa, the Colored American had a sea of bullshit surrounding him. He was oppressed by bullshit, mocked by bullshit, and lowered perceptually in *humanity ladder of greatness* by loads of bullshit (called science *then*). Yes, Harry, there is a lot of bullshit now[9] more than ever before. And of course, *bullshit perpetuates bullshit*. If there is so much bullshit around a person, then, when that person sees a lot of potently-affecting bullshit all around her then she has no option but "to continue to make assertions that purport to describe the way things are," however, that person is doing nothing but the creation of some more "bullshit."[10]

Now, the colored person is surrounded and faced by works of bullshitters. A load of bullshit that is harvested and heaped upon the Colored American has an enormous burden of *disgust* mixed with it. The colored person is regarded with implicitly covered nostrils. Nussbaum couldn't have described *the* disgusting situation (s) any better by arguing that disgust is a powerful emotion in many human beings. To be regarded as decent we have to brush everyday, shower everyday and inspect ourselves everyday lest we be seen as being *disgusting*. Nussbaum goes ahead and writes: "most societies teach the avoidance of certain groups of people as physically disgusting, bearers of contamination that the healthy element of society must keep at bay."[11]

And over the years, the Colored American has tried to either clean herself (through education), rationalized what is taken to be her *ontic disgust* (through religiousness and heart-felt discussion), or maintained that what is regarded as her *ontic disgust* is actually her misunderstood and misconceived, ontically authentic *Existentialist being*. A good number of the Colored Americans with substantial 'mentals'[12] and remarkable utility have tried over the years to let the world know that the Colored American is just like any other worldly Race; albeit with misplaced priorities. While the phenomenon of skin color is a contentious issue all over the world, its degree of contention is a gigantic point of *uneasiness* in North America. This is where color has remarkable instrumentality. W.E.B Dubois once wrote that

> After the Egyptian and Indian, the Greek and Roman, the Teuton and Mongolian, the Negro is a sort of seventh son, born with a veil, and gifted with second-sight in this American world,--a world which yields him no self-consciousness, but only lets him see himself through the revelation of the other world. It is a peculiar sensation, this double-consciousness, this sense of always looking at one's self through the eyes of others, of measuring one's soul by the tape of a world that looks on in amused contempt and pity.[13]

This is somewhat a position of disgust that puts the Colored American into two-minds: viewing herself through others' description of herself and also, seeing herself through her own conceptualization of her own self. The Colored American has slept in a position of Kantian *minority* for a long time. She's let others do *her* thinking and talking, for her, about her and against her.[14] Kantian concept of minority, as strictly applied to the colored person here, is the Colored American's sense of self from without. She has no say, practically speaking, as to what her sense of self from without means to her own self or others. She just feels it. Her sense of self from without is powerful; it is endearing and encroachingly effective and affective. The colored person finds herself with this sense of self that is both strange and unwelcome. But this sense of self is affective and however much the colored person wants to disown it, the potency of such an out-worldly branding is all too powerful. But the *branding* world doesn't only give the colored person a sense of self to grapple with and then leave her alone. The colored person is given a sense of self and then evaluated by the same sense of self giver:

> My body was given back to me sprawled out, distorted, recolored, clad in mourning in that white winter day. The Negro is an animal, the Negro is

bad, the Negro is mean, the Negro is ugly; look, a nigger, it's cold, the nigger is shivering, the nigger is shivering because he is cold, the little boy is trembling because he is afraid of nigger, the nigger is shivering with cold that goes through your bones, the handsome little boy is trembling because he thinks that the nigger is quivering with rage, the little white boy throws himself into his mother's arms; Mama, the nigger's going to eat me up.[15]

The colored person is given a terse, colorful description by the *brander*. The same given description is then analyzed not only by the brander but also by the colored person herself. This is because; around him is "a world that looks on in amused contempt and pity." However, the colored person doesn't accept this sense of self with ease. She rejects it somewhat. She tries to write her own self into acceptable sense of self. And how successful is she? The ones who are defeated are resigned into accepting the ridiculous like Randall Kennedy's Big Mama, who believed 'Niggers' are "discreditable Negroes."[16] This is the defeatist attitude of buying into what the brander wanted: self-description and destruction. Big Mama went as far as to say that she wouldn't allow a 'Nigger Doctor' to care for her. However, others don't show the same defeatist attitude:

> The history of the American Negro is the history of this strife,--this longing to attain self-conscious manhood, to merge his double self into a better and truer self. In this merging he wishes neither of the older selves to be lost. He does not wish to Africanize America, for America has too much to teach the world and Africa; he does not wish to bleach his Negro blood in a flood of white Americanism, for he believes--foolishly, perhaps, but fervently-- that Negro blood has yet a message for the world. He simply wishes to make it possible for a man to be both a Negro and an American without being cursed and spit upon by his fellows, without losing the opportunity of self-development.[17]

Now, the colored person seemed to be fending off the contempt and pity. She'd also been realistic and wise concerning the expectations she had. She wanted to shed off parts of her scales, not all. She too didn't want to 'Africanize America'. Oh, the colored person was starting to think? How dare she? Despite the outside sense of the perceived colored person's congenital *incapability*, she believed she could do something good for the world in order to be seen or accepted in a better light. The world *is* not easy on her though. Because the colored person's image was not an image created by the colored person herself then evaluated by the brander, she found herself mocked when she tried to negate the sense of self she'd been painted with.

She tried to procure a supposedly alien and estranging mode of self-expression and a surprising sense of self the branding heart found hard and bitter to swallow.

Some enslaved Colored Americans actually exerted their emotive strength and sense of dignity by defying the branding colonizers and slave masters.[18] That was thought stubbornly strange, stupid and futile. But that attempt bewildered the brander, nonetheless. The branding heart only expected a congenial colored person, a status quo accepting colored person; an economically productive handy woman. However, the Colored American knew the myopia of bad talk. The effect of *evil* talk of the less informed is always enormous but short-lived. She was sold into slavery by a person who either misunderstood her humanity or by a man who was scared of the very notion of the colored person's existential essence. The quiddity of *evil* is that its life span is as short as the imagination and memory of Alzheimer's patients.

The Colored American never gave up trying to be the woman she imagined herself to be. The brander intensified his war against the Colored American's struggle for sound and personalized objectivity of self: her 'innerity'.[19] But the colored woman intensified her soft, heart-warming human nature. She infected a section of the branding community with her then dismissed civility. The enlightened former branders started to *see* the real colored woman; the one who endures and rises above oppression without throwing in any blanket. The converted branders stood in line with her and said, at first: 'She's not one of us but she's just a normal human being.' The staunch, unrelenting branders frowned with so much disdain at the converted branders and said: "The weakness of your heart will let you imagine the *impossible*." And the '*impossible*' is the acceptability of the colored person's equal humanity; which was regarded as outright lunacy.[20]

The Colored American's sense of self became energized by the converted branders; her struggle for sound existence became semi-legitimized. She saw herself as having a good reason to match on with her *head high*. Then the converted branders increased the contents of their skulls (fuelled and stocked their 'mentals') and transition into this: 'She's just one of us.' The number of *we-are-all-equal crusaders* increased and the Colored American's hope increased. The entourage during the Colored American's match to sound sense of self included the Colored American herself and the converted branders.

Let's pause for a while! Let's go back for a *grain of knowledge* about the Colored American's path to dignified sense of self. Let me hope that such a postulate is not self-defeating. I believe a good fraction of the Colored America has attained some level of appreciable dignity. The Colored American has exerted her personhood whether we all agree with her assumed sense of self or not.

During slavery in America, the colored woman was seen as a tool, a menial entity that was weak mentally. Her 'mentals' was perceived as nonexistent. She was assumed to be in need of the guardianship or patronage of her master to survive. So she was regarded with heartbreaking patronization and condescension. It was assumed with a begrudging totality that her strength of will and sense of purpose would be lost in technology and development if the master was to let her go.[21] But the master wasn't so much worried about the tools, the Colored American, getting lost. The brander (master) was content with the assumption that civilization was something the Colored American couldn't grasp. He thought the Colored American would soon be lost in, and frustrated by, the massive technological complexity. The assumption was that the colored woman would never understand or sustain such an understanding even if she tried to understand technological complexities.

Pre-Emancipation Assumption: She'll soon come back to the plantation or she'll run to the bush where she belongs, if she walks free.

With this naïve sentiment, the master's sense of self (as conceptualized by the master himself) was never compromised. Well, that was what the master believed, unfortunately. However, the colored woman was misunderstood and underestimated. She however continued with the search for her sense of self through many *refined* attempts to find her place in America. She established her banks, churches, schools, stores;[22] and she participated in intellective scholarship with remarkable genius and strength of will. She fought in wars with exceptional valor and self-sacrifice, and used that *feeling* of self to profess a strong sense of African-Americanism or American-Africanism: "Bad Nigger" as colorless folks used to say then.[23] She was trying to end her *minority*. Kantian idea of minority if applied to the colored person best describes the colored woman's situation in America:

> It is difficult for the isolated individual to work himself out of the minority which has become almost natural for him. He has even become fond of it and for the time being is incapable of employing his own intelligence, because he has never been allowed to make an attempt.[24]

The colored person was starting to negate the essence of her minority. That became the problem as the master became uneasy with the new sense of strong Americanism in the colored woman. The traditional sense of the Colored American is that "nothing too Black nuh good" (anything that is too Black is not good)."[25] It is with the same understanding that Booker T. Washington inferred from the general belief that people assumed that "everything white was good and everything black was bad." He also understood from the general perception that god was assumed to be 'white' and devil 'black'.[26] And by 'nothing' it is meant the Colored American *herself*, not the blackness as *merely* the *color* in itself. "In the collective unconscious of *homo occidentalis*," Fanon writes, "the Negro—or, if one prefers, the color black—symbolizes evil, sin, wretchedness, death, war, famine."[27] With this assumed wretchedness, it is easy to see why the master frowned at any quest to emphasize Colored American's credible humanity.

We can't blame the bleaching poor souls that much because anything that is black is but "ugliness, sin, darkness, immorality."[28] No one will ever prefer the lowest echelon of humanity. Franz Fanon writes that the Negro is assumed to symbolize "the lower emotions, the baser inclinations, the dark side of the soul." You can't blame anyone who wants to run away from this wretchedness, this death, this famine, this war; can you?[29] Even as some Colored Americans were trying to let the master know that they're human, brave and intellectually competitive,[30] (Bigham, 86-91,2006) some Colored Americans believed they were disgusting and really wanted to get rid of the *self* that disgusted them, their blackness. Trying to act colorless, acting like Europeans and distancing oneself from anything African was prominent with some Colored Americans. Bleaching was one easy, innocent way of getting rid of the disgusting Africanness (blackness). So getting out of the minority situation was to get rid of the traditional view (the disgust and wretchedness view) of the Colored African. In the face of this monstrous branding and acceptable-sense-of-self opposition, the colored woman wanted to speak for herself, to define herself.

The freedom engendered by *emancipation* (Preliminary Emancipation Proclamation, September 1862 and 13th amendment, 1865)[31] was assumed (by the colorless master) it would lead to the demise of the colored person so as to come back to the master for help: the colored person's natural, determined niche. Freedom was also believed to, as argued above, lead to resurgence of 'animaliness' and natural Africanness of the Colored American.[32] But no, the colored person manifested a sense of self the master had either downplayed, ignored or suppressed. Having realized the emerging sense of self of the Colored American, the master became wary.

The master was then prompted to make sure that the colored person remained in the master's (and others') de-fined and enforced niche. The master had seen that the colored person wasn't going away, and she was challenging the very essence of the master's being. That embittered the master from head to toe. He mobilized and amassed all his power and influence to make sure that if the Colored American didn't go back to her natural *state of being* by natural means, then she had to be sent there by all means necessary. And the master had all the requisite, sublime political muscles and *will* to do so.

With the new-found sense of self-worth by the Colored American and the new realization by the master of a strong sense of self by the Colored American, the colored person was faced with new risks of going back to the same point she'd started from. She was no longer fighting for a sense of human dignity and self-worth. She was fighting to maintain the *real* part of her; the part the master feared and didn't want to accept. But the Colored American knew that such attitude of the master was and is always only but temporary. She'd been over that cycle a dozen times and she knew the weak nature of the master. The colored person was first perceived as not being able to do something appreciable civilization-wise. If she proved that wrong, a different, higher judgment point was sought.[33] Calibration demarcations kept shifting. The judgment point impressed in the form of something like the question: she can *do* it, but *how good?*[34]

Perhaps Toni Morrison won the Pulitzer Prize for *Beloved* only because she is both black and a woman.[35] It might also have been due to the campaign by egalitarians to help her win based on gender and Race but not necessarily on the quality of her work. If the preceding claims about Toni Morrison are true, then this is a good consolation to the Racists, branders and contemporary masters (capitalists). And just like Stephen Douglas once said, there will always be a position of inferiority and superiority in America racially speaking. Don't you just like how human beings' mentality works? Don't you just like how far branders can go to put the colored person down? In a way, this attitude is all too natural and it makes me sympathize with the branders against the unstoppable match of the colored person.

Now, for the Colored American, slavery started again but in a different form. Jim Crow came crashing down on her. Then soon segregation of the deadly form started (Between 1850-1910). The Colored American was no longer seen as weak and non-deserving in participation in civilization advancement because the colored person's customs "were in conflict with a civilization that he did not know and that imposed itself on him;" she was seen as *dangerous* and even more powerful when she got ahead or on par with the master. And for good reasons you can't argue with the apartheid South African government that defended Mandela's imprisonment by comparing him with Adolf Hitler. From being seen as a sub-human, Mandela's mental strength, humility, superior idealism and compassion changed the mentality of the brander's monstrosity of apartheid to give some *values* to Mandela. The values had to be tainted by being associated with someone abhorrent: Hitler. The colored person used to have no value, but now she had values but those values were 'dark and dangerous.'[36] In all corners of the earth the colored person was sexually dangerous to the innocent and civilized colorless woman.[37] The master's stomach growled with fright. 'No, that won't happen!'

Because the colored person didn't change but the circumstances around her did, she endured through the new slavery. Then the circle of the brander became divided again and the Colored American sensed a mass of colorlessness next to her. Her spirit lit up with divine essence. Again, the circle of converts started to balloon; the number of crusaders increased. Her fights in wars and poking of her nose into different aspects of American life became a significant problem to the bad and the hard-core colorless person. The fight on both sides started, again. This time the Colored American was no longer seen as inferior in essence. She was assumed inferior pretentiously by the brander to make her being excluded from the anal of American society and her vilification both easy and warranted. It became a war both intellectually emotive and physically vicious.

Having talked about the colored person's struggle toward appreciable sense of personhood, one has to think critically about the events of August 29, 2005.

> The story of Hurricane Katrina as originally constructed served authoritarianism, racism and a generally grim view of human nature. It was first told hysterically, as though New Orleans had been hit by a torrent of poor black people or had become, as Maureen Dowd of the *New York*

Times put it then, "a snake pit of anarchy, death, looting, raping, marauding thugs." An overwrought *Huffington Post* columnist even spread rumors of cannibalism, while many major media outlets repeated rumors of snipers firing on helicopters. These rumors were never substantiated, but they interfered with the rescue operations.[38]

However much she struggles through all odds to regain her ancestral essence and refinement, history never leaves the colored person. Even now, whatever she does is still characterized into historically known niche. She's not always perceived as closer to the revered side of humanity, and no moral regard and care is taken when she's being evaluated and dissected.

During Hurricane Katrina, she was always assumed the first, or the only one, to loot. She was not naturally inclined to help others; so it was assumed. The credit of all the good things she does goes to the decent *man* who teaches her to be good.

And Hurricane Katarina reflects so much on the sense of self of the colored person from *without*. The sense of self of the Colored American that comes from her own self-worth is nonexistence *by* the mainstream America. When the colored person was the 'rescuee' the media and *land* projected the rescuer as a good-hearted American. When the Colored American was the rescuer, she was projected as an indecent, insensitive looter. Don't you just like the social corruption and insecurity of the brander?

> The evidence these journalists overlooked was everywhere. In September 2005, Malik Rahim, the ex–Black Panther who co-founded Common Ground Relief and who lives in the Algiers neighborhood, told Amy Goodman of *Democracy Now!* on camera about vigilante murders of black men. He showed her the body of a dead black man lying under a sheet of corrugated metal, bloated and decaying in the heat.[39]

There it is! However, it has to be noted that the average Colorless American, while having his own historical, personal and unconscious prejudices, he's not supposed to be blamed in excess of what he's truly culpable for. And it is in this vein that we can agree with what Omaroseonee Manigault-Stallworth said in Jet Magazine on April 12,

2004 about the media portrayal of the colored person: "Historically, blacks have been portrayed negatively on reality television. We don't come across well. You've got to start looking and saying, 'Is that really how all blacks are?' Because they are trying to say that this is representative of our people." Great culpability lies with the doctoring of information by the media and the powerful people of the land who masquerade as true 'valuers' of humans of all kinds.

If the Colored American is projected as dangerous and anti-social, there is no reason why the average, less-informed Colorless American would welcome the anti-social or associate with the looter; a 'threat' to his livelihood and his family. That *about* makes sense. The historical sense of self of the Colored American from without is therefore reinforced for the comfort of the brander, and the innocent, face-value application by the average, less-informed and misled *Colorless America*.

The unconscious entry of the colored person's conceptualization by the colorless person is therefore aided in emergence and inculcated into the minds of the average colorless person. The colorless person is only but protecting his property from the *Statutory Bad Person*: the colored person. While the average, fearful colorless man shares in the blame, he's prompted into vigilance by the media.

> Real people got caught in the crossfire. Take Donnell Herrington, a 33-year-old former Brink's truck driver who stayed behind to help his grandparents and who later rescued many others by boat from their flooded housing project. Herrington was walking to the evacuation site in Algiers Point when a white vigilante with a shotgun attempted to murder him. Herrington was shot in the neck, hit so hard the blast lifted him off the ground, and then shot again in the back as he tried to escape. His friend and cousin, who were walking with him, were also injured by the buckshot and then chased down by racists who terrorized them. An African-American couple in the neighborhood drove Herrington to the nearest hospital…[40]

The shooting colorless people aren't necessarily Fundamental Racists, but they were promoted into acting in a Racist manner by the doctoring media and personalities.

Now, the reader shouldn't take these quotes at face value nor should she dismiss them as commonly American and insignificant. The historical evaluation and positioning of the colored person is always invoked in times of needs. The brander discards morality, modesty and civility at such times. He loses his sense and essence in the assumed badness of the colored person. Moral observance is ignored because the overwhelming badness is encroaching.

This invokes the significance of colorlessness in post-independent Jamaica "where Governments have largely ignored the Black heroes like Nanny of the Maroons, Sam Sharpe, Paul Bogle, and Marcus Garvey, and instead have constantly promoted the White heroes Norman Manley, Alexander Bustamante, and George William Gordon…"[41] This is hardly surprising, however, one has to be reminded about the historical continuation of such sense of uncertainty of blackness emergence and also, the less understood nature of Africanness (blackness).

The new sense of self by and of the Colored American is a point of *uneasiness* to the Colorless American. What is remarkable is that any Mary or John can find consolation support for his or her claims against the African person worldwide. When I read this book, *In defense of Elitism*, by William Henry III, I find this same uneasiness (perhaps with good intentions or boldness) throughout the book. To downplay the achievements of the colored person, quality and merit-wise, on some assumed empirical social facts, reminds me of the 1920s and 1930s Race debate. Henry argues that August Wilson was given the Pulitzer Prize by the jury because he was a high school dropout. He assumed, or perhaps the jury members told him, that the jury was *attracted* by the fact that Wilson was a high school dropout.[42] Henry doesn't consider the possibility that, despite being a high school dropout, Wilson's play was the *best*. And of course, if Henry is defending elitism, he would do everything to keep the status quo: *colorless only, or colored with exception*. Let me be presumptuous for a reason because Henry is pro-elitism.

Because the means by which the Colored American was vilified are becoming increasingly limited, opportunities such as defending 'elitism' or Hurricane Katarina present very valuable tools to the brander and the 'vilifier'. The brander and the vilifier revisits the past they were not part of and, perhaps, wanted to be part of but couldn't. Now, those hearts, who romanticize about the glories of the past, get to have something to fall back to. And the media is there to back them up. Evolutionary biologist, Richard Dawkins, has helped us understand in *The God Delusion* that a sense of self can transcend everything one feels even with people we can call the educated minds. Dawkins explains to us how highly educated people, in the United States, can sometimes be wary of declaring themselves 'atheists' because of the possible bad sentiments from their families. Even with PhDs and the ability to defend their unbelief or belief with clarity in intellective engagement, and teaching in the country's highest institutions, how they felt about themselves was the overriding factor and to some extent, even immune to any highest level of education.

The sense of self in the Americas (both colored and colorless) played and still plays a role in inter-racial intercourses, discourses and existence. The elevated sense of self of the colorless person has very much affected the colored person to feel less human. Any attempt by the colored person to come clean and hold her head high is fought with understandable but subtle fury by the colorless America to make sure that historical flaws (both real and invented) are maintained. It is good to point out that the assumed *badness/immoral nature* of the Colored American (in history and now) is tied to her 'blackness'. The nature of the colored person herself and the color that describes her are seen as one and the same without any critical analysis. We will discuss this comprehensively in Chapter Two; especially, section 2.2.

1.3 The Colored African

Like her cousins in the Americas, the Colored African is both humbled and bitter. She's the cradle of civilization; the first 'modern' woman.[3] Indeed, she wonders if that means anything at all. She's the

---

[3] This is still a smart attempt to debase the colored person. See Dawkins, *River out of Eden*, p.52

first woman; *far* in lineage from her ancestors but she's still considered the savage. She wonders why she's no much body hair like the wild primates. She wonders why her hair is not straight like her simian ancestors. Her hair is so curly and nappy that only a lost soul would consider her close to any primates. No animal is close to her either. She too wonders why her lips are pronounced, unlike those of her ancestors who had or have lipless mouths. She also wondered why her nose is beautifully broad unlike the simian ancestors who had and have *flat, sunk-in noses*. And she wonders why she's not technologically advanced like the rest of the world: the colored world (the yellow person; the brown person; the red person), the colorless person and every person there is. And she above all wonders why she's forgiving and humble in the face of all the atrocious and monstrous deeds hurled her way over the years, centuries.

She has humane and humanity-uniting values and morality defining tenets: humility, sincere forgiveness, and inability to inflict suffering on others without compunction. Are such virtues primitive or evolutionarily advanced? There are, in true existential honesty, no appreciable (if there are) virtues in the wild! Peter Singer would perhaps or definitely disagree.[43] We can understand Singer's position as disciplinarily necessary and modest; highly interpretive, questionable but understandable.

The rest, both colored and colorless, regard her with sorrow and spite. In Africa, the person of color is viewed with a sense of compassion and disdain with an external, objective point of view. The point of view is objective because the brander assumes an overwhelmingly coherent and potent (scientifically authenticated) position relative to Africa. And for all reasons he has a point: science (tested, controlled, multiply-and-independently-verified proof) and empiricism (everyday intuitive observations).

The colonizing Europe perceived and instrumentalized the instrumentality of what they thought as human-like Africans. But the Colored African was confused by many things. Some branders were compassionate, humble and loving; while others were as ruthless and as wild as heartless lions after their preys. The brander was as hairy as the simian creatures she was assumed to be closer to. The brander was also lipless like the simian creatures in the wild. The brander too had hair that was as long as the hair of the horse's tail. And above all, the colorless European was aggressive and animal-like (merciless) in the treatment of the Colored African. However, the Colored African couldn't match the technological advance of the brander. The brander was far ahead technology-wise that to say the brander was closer to the simian cousins than the Colored African was seemingly fatuitous—an unthinkable proscription. The Colored African saw the ape-likeness of the brander but 'sushed'! *You have no case in the face of technology, science and arts*. And it is with good reason that Steve Bantu Biko, in *Cry Freedom*, wondered:

> When I was a student, I suddenly realized that it wasn't just the job I was studying for that was white. The history we read was made by white men, written by white men. Television, medicine, cars...all invented by white men. Even football. In a world like that, it is hard not to believe that there is something inadequate about being born black.[44]

And we can all agree with (not accept) that dilemma somewhat. Biko didn't think hard enough. The brander too had a long, pointed nose unlike his simian neighbours who had and have flat noses. Such existential inconsistences confused the Colored African. However, she was still beneficial to the brander.

The Colored African had giant, industrious muscles and the brander saw them beneficial. A strong African, then, was an economic tool. A gullible African, now, is a capitalist pool.

The Colored African is placed in a position she doesn't agree with. She too doesn't engender a strong sense of everlasting mockery and defiance against the procured stigmatism. The colonizer, another big brander, categorized the Colored African without falsifying his real disdain of the African personhood, and also, the starting and defiant Africanism. The brander did and still does the branding with so much confidence and fervent belief that the Colored African is at times lost in the process of authenticating or evangelizing her real sense of self. The brander assumed a requisite *immorality* for a 'good' cause: sinking the Colored African into decadence and, more seriously, claimed 'moral necessity' out of it. But how does the brander, who commits unspeakable horrors against the Colored African, live with himself? Sam Harris has the answer from the deeds of the Nazi Germany guards, who saw Jews as not "being objects of his moral concern."[45] The brander, like the Nazi guards, has beliefs that "inured him to the natural human sympathies that might have otherwise prevented such behaviour."[46] Completely absolved and shorn of moral considerations, the brander could then regard and treat the Colored African in any way he thought fit. The branding was done with so much wisdom and craftiness that the Colored African stared in awe and helplessness.

The Colored African became even afraid to reject the stereotype, the blackness (branding) and she acted like the Sartre's Jew: "They [the Jews] have allowed themselves to be poisoned by the stereotype that others have of them, and they live in fear that their acts will correspond to this stereotype."[47] And this reminds me of an article I read online in 2002 or 2003. I can't, unfortunately, locate the article. It was about an accomplished Colored American University Chemistry professor, who said that he was careful in all the things he did because any one mistake would smear the whole Race. Despite being good in his field, being a full professor and a head of his department, he still felt the weight of his assumed inadequacy. I bet he assumed it was care, prudence and responsibility. He was a colored person, but who told him he repressented the whole Race? He'd be delusional if he assumed he represented the Race. The stereotype has drained into his blood-stream like the fear of the Sartre's Jews. And I agree with William Henry III when he lashed out against affirmative action and excessive political correctness that: "One's worth and self-regard ought to come from individual competitive performance, not group identity." If the professor believed in his abilities, he'd not worry about making mistakes. He should not also think he's a 'black professional,' because he's just a professional man. Pure and simple! You can see what branding does to the mind! I circumstantially failed some university courses in McGill, and if any colorless person assumed it's because of my Race, then, I would gladly group them in the same delusion with the Colored American professor. And if I brooded over the fact that I failed because it would factually substantiate the racial stereotype, then I would go in as delusional as well. Many of my colored brothers and sisters (Africans, Caribbean and Americans) were getting 'As' from the same courses I failed. I hope you get the point.

Our Colored American chemistry professor is like some of his cousins in the original colored continent. First, there was the Colored African who was so much taken in by the branding of the colonizer that s-he was resigned to the fact that she was who she'd been argued to be. She accepted that position with remarkable humility. She was so content with her caricatured self that the brander *rebranded* her, not as the initial caricatured self, but as a different one; a progressive, civilized woman of color; weird looking but politically acceptable. I guess the *rebranded* Colored African realized she couldn't beat the brander so she joined him. Anthony Lambede writes:

> Some Alien subjects become dupe of such sinister propaganda and consequently become tools or instruments of imperialism for which great service they are highly praised by the imperialistic power and showered with such epithets as "cultured", "liberal", "progressive", "broadminded" etc.[48]

This speaks of what was and is still required of the Colored African. She's supposed to conform to the created realities about and for her. Countering the created (concocted) nature of the Colored African was (and still is) the father of hostility towards the Colored African. Good-hearted colorless hearts became targets of mockery when they joined the colored person in the fight against the caricatured nature of the Colored African. Whatever she thought of herself was assumed to be a grave detriment civilization-wise. Although still maintained presently, the methods and intentions are disguised.

The vigor with which the Colored African created sense of self was and is fought off (by both the colored and the good-hearted colorless folks) amazes the Colored African herself. She tried, and still tries, to portray with humble, innocuous utilities to the brander, the real Colored African. The brander's view of the Colored African is this: "The display of Blacks in colonial expositions aimed primarily to prove to Western visitors that Africans were savages to be civilized by the Empire."[49] While this appears to be an ancient view that might not be applicable now, there are many areas of our contemporary Africanness where this 'savageness' of the African can be perceptually assumed or sensed. Somalia has been left to rot by the West. Rwandan in 1994 is a paradigm case of Africa seen through the ancient lenses in our present age. Civilians in Darfur have been left to the mercy of a warlord because, well, they are Africans. And this can also be seen in how some authors have tried to contextually downplay what King Leopold II did in the Congo in the middle to the end of 1800s (Hochschild, 1998). This is argued with the reasoning that King Leopold II's intention wasn't the extermination of the ethnic African people, but a murderous adventure necessitated by his economic interest in Congo as his personal possession, not Belgium's colony. When Rafael Lemkin coined the word GENOCIDE to describe the killing of people based on their ethnicity, religion and nationality, he didn't intent it to mean that the killing has to be primarily the intention. Regardless of the intention, the inflectional killing based on Limkin's definition is genocide.[50]

When the Colored African tried to counter this view, the brander became surprised. The brander either laughed or fumed; nothing in between. However, the laughter of the brander was not innocent. It was always followed by a-well-thought-out application of draconian steel. The target *is* always the *head* of the Colored African.[51] It's the head of the Colored African; the head that'd in history (naively initially) been thought to contain no substantially productive white matter. Since the head now has some functional white substance, it is targeted pointedly with a hard hand of the fearful brander. This way, the Colored African would not think or imagine something that'd be detrimental to the brander's assumed 'naturalness.' This naturalness is the entitlement to every *good* there is on earth: every refined innovation, every required normative civility.

Either the Colored African has no acknowledged place in history because of his undeserving nature as a person fit for civilization, or she's ignored because she'd not contributed anything appreciably substantial to the world development-wise. And Fannon writes: "I came into the world imbued with the will to find a meaning in things, my spirit filled with the desire to attain the source of the world, and then I found that I was an object in the midst of other objects."[52] The colored person is faced by *whatsis* of her own self (enforced by forced self-reflection) not by the ambitious project she intended to use to understand the world or stock her 'mentals' and make it operative.

But the Colored African was not at all assumed to be of the same breed she'd been assumed to be in the past. There were many breeds with different intellective and emotive capacities. All of which were normatively different in the eyes of the brander. There was that group that was not *progressive*; a group that was assumed stubborn. This breed was a breed whose vilification, contrary to the brander's intentions, led to the strengthening of spirit and resolves of the Colored African. The stubborn Colored African was abused and 'door-matted' but she felt superior to the brander whose aggressive sentiment was stirred by a feeling of inadequacy. She was fought with technologically advanced gadgets and socially clever methods, but she easily understood the mentality of the brander. The brander was only acting *natural*: protecting his misunderstood or understood but misappropriated Darwinian niche.

However, this assumed natural state of being of the brander was assumed to be the protection of purity and superiority of the brander. This sense of purity and superiority was interpreted by the stubborn Colored African as brander's feeling of inadequacy; and simply, a natural fear stemming from the average colorless brander. Any attempt to present the Colored African as insignificant led to the very idea of vocal and mental muscularity of the stubborn Colored African. The emotively helpless brander, having exhausted all the options to quiet the mentally muscled Colored African, went to the extreme. The extremity the brander reached only explained the significance of the mentally muscled Colored African: she's an unsung victor in every sense. She wasn't melting into the mine fields of South Africa, or getting lost on the 'White' highlands of Kenyan or the dense forests of Mozambique. *She was here, she's here, and she'll be here.*

But who was the mentally muscled Colored African? Why did the brander fear her? What did she say? One was cited earlier (Lambede) and the second will be cited here. Let's see why the mentally muscled Colored African was always melted away as fear clouded the brander's anachronistic perception of the Colored African. Steve Biko wrote in, 'The Quest for a True Humanity', *I write what I like* (1978), that

> Black consciousness is an attitude of the man and a way of life, the most positive call to emanate from the black world for a long time. Its essence is the realisation by the black man of the need to rally together with his brothers around the cause of oppression—the blackness of their skin—and to operate as a group to rid themselves of the shackles that bind them to perpetual servitude. [53]

I will ignore Biko's use of 'black' and 'blackness' for I don't understand the insight as to why he accepted the brander's description. However, the content of the quote is timelessly rich and mighty. The Colored African is told by the mentally muscled Colored African that she's a person with ontic significance not the idealized caricature. The person in the Colored African is advised that she's a potential intellectual innovator and futuristic significance.

This, history always proves. It has to be noted that the Colored African has always known in her ontic past that there's *no* mortal being *over and above* her ontic being. But the realities and the force the brander's voice exerted impressed negatively on the majority of the colored Africa to believe the brander's fabrications. The Colored African has not written her history in an appreciably descent mode. She's not advanced socially, scientifically and technology in a comparable manner. She's little to show but a lot of historical contextualization to be par. This is frustrated, however, by empirical support leading to the claim that she's the lower echelon of the hierarchized *homo sapiens* (having *not* caught up with the rest of the family) but the upper echelon of the hierarchy of the other *hominidae* (as she can do more than the rest of *hominidae* except other *homo sapiens*). This is a position advanced also by Moses Maimonides in *The Guide of the Perplexed* ('the parable of the palace'). This can be found in Book III, chapter 51 of the book. Maimonides also included Turks among the 'monkeys'.

> Such are the extreme Turks that wander about in the north, the Kushites who live in the south, and those in our country who are like these. I consider these are irrational beings, and not as human beings they are below mankind, but above monkeys, since they have the form and shape of man, and a mental faculty above that of a monkey.[54]

Kushites is translated as 'Negroes' in some translations. What the brander said (says) made (makes) a lot of sense because the brander had (has) established a position that some Colored Africans took (take) for a divine essence. A university educated colleague and a friend of mine once told me that there must be some advantage god has given 'white people.' The Colored African lost (loses) herself and defined herself by what the brander said (says). Her image is distorted;[55] the self-esteem thrown into the loony bin. And Gerard Prunier couldn't have said it any better when he wrote that "The Europeans rationalized African cultures to death. And it is that contrived rationality that they bequeathed to Africa when they walked away from the continent in the 1960s."[56] What Africans and Africa became was not incidental, but intentionally monstrous. The only significance many Colored Africans ripped was a sense of instrumentality to the brander; the economic industriousness. The Colored African at least had one way, in that regard, in which she had some ontically appreciated value. The empirical manifestation of the brander's social advance and the visibility of the brander's success overwhelmed the Colored African to accept the status quo.

While the empirical realities of the brander's success didn't need reinforcement, the brander tried to make his status sublime and psychologically affecting to the Colored African. Biko once wrote that 'At the heart of this kind of thinking is the realization by blacks that the most potent weapon in the hand of the oppressor is the mind of the oppressed."⁵⁷ The Colored African had to be controlled and put down, degraded so as to safeguard the brander's imperial longevity. Once the mind of the Colored African was controlled, any black (black as in bad) political trick meant to put her down worked with remarkable profundity. Many duped Colored Africans sought approval from the brander by joining the merciless oppression of their fellow siblings. This was common during Apartheid South Africa, King Leopold Congo Free State, and many parts of colonial Africa where collaboration with colon-ial masters was rewarded. And a paradigmatic example is the colonial Kenya with Mau Mau. Wole Soyinka, in his 1986 Noble Prize acceptance speech, writes: "The inner ring of guards, the blacks, moved in, lifted the bodies by hooking their hands underneath the armpits of the detainees, carried them like toads in a state of petrification to one side, divided them in groups."⁵⁸ He continued:

> The faces of the victims are impassive; they are resolved to offer no resistance. The beatings begin: one to the left side, then the back, the arms - right, left, front, back. Rhythmically. The cudgels swing in unison. The faces of the white guards glow with professional satisfaction, their arms gesture languidly from time to time, suggesting it is time to shift to the next batch, or beat a little more severely on the neglected side. In terms of images, a fluid, near balletic scene.⁵⁹

This is the manifestation of the empowering emotions (professional satisfaction) of the colorless guards; and the disempowering emotions (pain) of the victims of *cudgels* and *professional satisfaction*. The oppression was exacerbated by the duped Colored Africans ('black' guards).

It therefore became the duty of the mentally muscled Colored Afric-an to enlighten the mentally duped Colored African that she's signific-ant not only to herself and the myopic brander, but also, to the world. The mentally duped Colored African was reminded that the brander w-as successful because he tried, and she was advised to pick herself up with the same ancestral resilience, pride, kindness and valor to enforce or re-enforce her place in the face of the brander's hostility.⁶⁰ The 'bla-ck' (African) consciousness evangelists weren't telling the mentally dup-ed Colored African that she had to claim what wasn't there or that she had to invent who she should be; the mentally muscled colored African was telling the mentally duped Colored African to reinforce her almost forgotten 'Africanness.'[61] The Colored African was advised to go back to her *pre-color-significance* era (assumed error) and be just an African that was to adapt, with a respectable self, to the realities of the changing world around her…just like the brander has.

I leave it open as to whether or not the Colored African has scaled off the monstrously caricatured Africanness. Since Africa is still divided in the claim for supremacy, with the Colored African and the Colorless African claiming the anachronistic superiority, it'll be left to the curious and the intellectual to decide.

However, I'll have to say as I close this chapter that our simple human nature makes me certain that the sense of self of and by the colored person is still questioned. The brander is not a person of the past; he's a person existing *over* time. He's gone through evolutionary process and the ease with which he can be safely spotted is becoming difficult under normal circumstances. And at times, the colored person herself unknowingly joins in the branding of her own self. At times she doesn't know the self-destructiveness of such self-afflictions; at times she knows the consequences but has no choice in so acting. And by all reasons, the existing brander is always the one with macabre self-esteem disguised as supremacy. As we can see from the preceding discussion, the Colored American and the Colored African are trying hard to be recognized. There's a general, unfounded fear of the Colored Africanness. I will leave it open whether or not the euro-standardized world is really ready to accept with scientific honesty the true nature of the Colored personhood.

CHAPTER TWO

Blackness and Whiteness Ontically Speaking

IN chapter one, we discussed both the present and the historical struggles of the colored person. What upsets me so much is how the world has just accepted whatever Europe dictates without any critical analysis. We have seen that people in our euro-standardized world together with people of African descent don't take 'blackness' only as a description of who they are, they have taken it to be who they are *per se*. In other words, they have become so much attached, enamored and defined by blackness that they have gone to the extent of owning and defending blackness *per se*. Anyone who abuses black things, which are traditionally known to be *bad* raises colored people's eye brows. We will see in this chapter how colored people have gone to the extent of defending blackness in itself as good. When a person argues that a *black cat* is a sign of bad luck, colored people get upset. Their only connection with the cat is blackness forgetting the fact that we are talking about a cat; an animal. They get upset because blackness not only describes them; it is who they see themselves to be. The blackness of the cat is also literal not symbolic.

This phenomenon is not only restricted to colored people. People of European descent have become so much attached to the color white that the thought that there can be a separation between who they are *per se* and the color white makes them wonder. Whiteness is considered pure and a symbol of godliness so it is understandable why Europeans wanted and want to be described white. However, it is not understand-dable (to me at least) why being described as white is required to exalt one's sense of self. In this chapter, I will present whiteness and black-ness and how Europeans and people of European descent and African and people of African descent have owned them respectively.

2.1 Historical Backdrop

We've discussed in *chapter one* how a sense of self of the colored person has been affected. However much the colored person tried to fend off the branding of the brander, his conscience became overwhelmmed by the empirical realities and she, to some extent, became resigned to the fact that she's less of a remarkable human being than the brander.

When the Moors (colored) enslaved both colored and colorless people, a sense of perceived inferiority had nothing to do with the color of the skin. George Fredrickson, in *Racism: a brief history*, presented a position that the average contemporary person doesn't always hear.[1] When the Christians in Europe regarded the colored Ethiopians with high regard both socially and religiously, a sense of superiority wasn't so much about the color, but about the social, moral and religious import of the person in question.[2] This pre-contemporary Racism period is also portrayed by Curt Keim in his book, *Mistaking Africa*. He writes that "In ancient Greece and Rome, race does not seem to have been a significant issue."[3] Keim explains how differences in skin color were only perceived as a result of geographical domicile rather than a ground for racial subordination and subjugation. It has also been noted that Europeans benefited from African trade products (gold, ivory etc.) and ideas through Arab intermediaries from the 7th century.[4]

This same issue can be found also in Bacon's Rebellion in the colonial America. Domestic servants were both colored and colorless. The rebellion brought about the color rather than the then existing class differences. European-American domestic servants were replaced with

African slaves. This not only started the oppression of the Colored American, it also instigated discrimination based on skin color.[5] (See AAA video)

However, when the colored person lost power, and the colorless person gained immeasurable power, the colored slavery was maintained and the colorless slavery was done away with gradually for a purpose; which I assume with no risk of controversy, is understandable. The shift in power and the arrogance of the Ethiopian Christians brought the doom (maybe) to the colored Race in Christendom. This is the beauty of Christianity, isn't it? Christianity became instrumental in 'authenticating' the existential and metaphysical position of the colored person. Latter developments such as Transatlantic Slave Trade, Colonialism and Darwinian Theory of Evolution had a lot of impact on placing the African personhood under the doormat. However much the colored person tried to lift herself up and out of the maze of both real and fabricated image of her self, she found her defiant self costly. The zeal of the brander was strengthened by remarkably grounded, powerful piety and political traditions.

The irony of the colored person's struggle for solace and freedom is striking. Many colored persons found refuge in the brander's religion; another *tool* that further degraded the colored person in the eyes of the brander.[6] But the colored person's sense of self as a lower form of humanity was reinforced at many levels. As some sections of the colored population started to abandon their traditional, meaningful ways of life, they embraced the brander's ways of life. They disowned themselves as 'savages' but still expected the brander to respect the same selves they dubbed archaic, and personally disowned. That was strikingly stupid, but interesting. The colored person started to see her ways as remote and archaic. She started to crib a completely vilifying foreignness. The crib-bing started to reinforce her status as a lower human form whose ways of life; spiritual and social, were anti-civilization. The colored person didn't know that by abandoning her way of life, she'd abused who she *is* not who she *was*.

Mid-Thought Pause: Don't expect respect for your way of

life if you've disowned it.

Having seen the colored person had disowned her way of life, the brander started to giggle in private with superior satisfaction. However, in the presence of the confused colored person, the brander put a pretentious garland of significance on the duped colored person. The brander acted with pretentious precocity. With persecution and vilification into social decadence, the colored person assumed the man with the *cross* was not part of the brander's circle: the men with the flag and the chain.

However, the mentally-muscled Colored African soon realized that the *cross* and the *flag* were two facets of the same imperial entity: oppression (vilification). Yet the mentally- duped Colored African was beguiled and sucked into pretension unknowingly by a well-designed façade projected in an emotionlessly religious tone. The colored person therefore joined the crusade leading to her own destruction. *And she still wonders why her ways are considered devilish and her place the lowest echelon of humanity?* As she denounced her spiritual being, she denounced herself unknowingly, perhaps knowingly having been duped. Her adopting foreign spirituality was meant to tell her that everything she naturally exuded was of no value. The 'good men' were telling the colored person that disowning Africanness was the salvation: salvation from her own self symbolized by her 'blackness'. And what was even more frustrating was the fact that she was asked to disown her spirituality for delusional claims of a son of a Jewish carpenter from a remote land.

The same foreign spirituality did a lot more. As the colored person would later learn, the brander's way of life wasn't as sublime, truthful and moral as it was presented. It is to be understood that the first use of Africans as slaves for larger commercial purposes was started with full support of the *pope* in 1518 in Spain under King Charles I.[7] What a shame! Papal blessing of slaves' purchase was also instrumental in Portugal. It is also important to remember that the slaves were not only 'pure' Africans, but included, Turks, Moors etc. American Indians were enslaved in America and some also sold to Spain.[8] So far *a* man of god (Pope) endorsed the sale of human beings to oppression and degrade-ation. And Bertrand Russell has put this papal shame and devilishness beautifully:

> The churches, as everyone knows, opposed the abolition of slavery as long as they dared, and with a few well-advertised exceptions they opposed at the present day every movement toward economic justice. The pope has officially condemned Socialism.[9]

As the colored person tried to delight in the new found spirituality, she fell into a 'igger[4] trap; the trap she'd been required to fall into for so long were it not for the grits of her resilient spirit. The brander knew the colored person doesn't only have the grits and valor of the lioness, but also, timeless patience, goodness of heart[10] and perseverance.

The brander had to therefore make sure that the colored person was combated in all spheres of civilized colorless existence. The men of god were also recruited for mental softening of the colored person. If men of go-d whom the colored person had confided in told her she was a *lower* human form, she'd have nothing to say but believe what the *lord god* had decreed through the mouths of his/her servants: the colorless priests (and by designed-nature god is colorless for fairness). The colorless priest was so congenial and ostensibly gentle not to be the ultimate truth-sayer. It was written, as the good book dictates, by lord god that the colored person was destined to be the servant of the rest of the colorless and the less colored worlds.[11] The colored persons were considered "h-ewers of woods and carriers of water."[12] Who could doubt the ingenuity of the brander?

Mid-Thought Pause: Fight a strong and savvy enemy in all fronts with all you've got!

Christianity, which the colored person has embraced, is the instigator of her oppression over the years. It instilled in the minds of many

---

[4] You can call it a 'Nigger Trap' or a 'Bigger Trap, 'either way, it serves its purpose.

(including the colored person herself) an indelible mark of eternal misperception and hate of self-identification by the colored self.[13]

In the next section we'll see how the brander had made the colored person hate herself. The caricaturing of the colored self became a successful macabre campaign for a successful evangelism of the colored person's journey to the perceptual, lowest societal echelon. What you believe is what you do the best. Colored people who believed the negative evangelism of their sense of self aided the campaign that led to their perceptual inferior status. They aided this either by embracing the negative and immoral caricatures, or by disowning their natural Africanness.

2.2 Blackness

Black is Beautiful? I will fault the beginning of *Songs of Solomon* (Chapter 1 verses 5&6) for this out of context, misleading derivation by commentators. The statement, *I am Black but comely*, appears at the begining of Songs of Solomon (Chapter 1, verse 5). However, *Black is Beautiful* (1) and *I am Black but comely* (2) (Which also means *I am black but beautyful*) don't mean the same thing and don't convey the same message. The latter is destroyed by 'but.' *I am Black and Beautiful* (3) would have been better than *I am Black but Beautiful*. However, qualifying the beauty of the colored person implies the opposite or mocks the beauty being qualified. Simply say *I am beautiful* (well, if you're beautiful then I'll see it so you need not say that). However, the latter is better. Separating the colored self and the beauty undermines the claim of beauty inherent in the colored self. Qualifying the beauty of the colored person gives an impression something is being enforced; something that isn't inherent in that supposedly beautiful self. It has to be remembered also that there is *no* such a thing as *a* colored beauty or colorless beauty strictly speaking. There are colored beauties and colorless beauties. Beauty shouldn't be taken as a collective possession of a single, standard group; it is a quality of individuals. I have to admit that physical similarities through Humean relation of ideas impress on us strongly that we see beauty as a quality of a class rather than individuals. No two people can have the same level of beauty. Beauty is *one* as a quality of all entities. Its manifestation, however, is different. These varied manifestations allow us to talk of beauties rather than beauty. So when we talk of all extant entities, we are talking of BEAUTY, but if we pick individual entities, we can talk of beauties in form of variants. I see no contradiction there. However, this concept can be confusing. You can classify a given BEAUTY on racial bases for the sake of identification not subordination; as *I am black but beautiful* implies.

Now, 2 above is difficult to understand. Even more frustrating is the fact that I don't actually know the meaning of 1. I've tried, on many occasions, to contextualize the meaning of those words. I first took 1 as a metaphor meaning the skin of the Colored African or that the person of African descent is beautiful. I assumed the parties that coined or are using the phrase have a level of intellect to utilize the phrase as a metaphor. That, I think, on my part, is a safe and sensible assumption. I call it a metaphor because not all the Colored Africans have the literal black skin if at all we have Africans with literal black skin. The closer the pigmentation is to blackness the better the assumption of blackness works. In other words, the claim for blackness works if the skin color is closer to blackness; just like my skin which can pass for blackness.

However, the color metaphor or color symbolism wasn't restricted to pigmentation description. It has been used by the colored person to symbolize a sense of identity and personhood. Blackness has been perfectivized, purified and 'significated' to make it workable for the colored person's sense of self and identity. Anything the colored person did and still does is christened 'black'. Steve Biko once wrote that "being black is not a matter of pigmentation—being black is a reflection of mental attitude."[14] A sense of empowerment through the workings of the mind of the colored person, in Biko's case, is made significant by making blackness (not Africanness, but assumed so) a positive phenomenon. This application of blackness to all aspects of the colored person's life just fits in like *lock and key* into what the brander wanted the colored person to be: black literally (ontically) and figuratively.

Objectification or instrumentalization of all aspects of the colored person of African descent therefore became the invigoration of *blackness* and *emasculation* of the African personhood. Blackness became fortified to create a sense of meaning and racial identity. Blackness became dear to the Colored African. The Colored African became so attached to blackness that reverence of blackness almost became a divinization of blackness: to be proud of a sense of self of the colored person was to be proud of being *black*; to associate inseparably and divinely with blackness. This is why religious people like Louis Farrakhan and Elijah Mohammed of *Nation of Islam* try to metaphysically and 'divinely' make sense of their blackness by arguing that everything comes out from blackness. There seems to be some consolation, to the thought-less, in the postulate that god is black. Farrakhan writes:

> How could God make Himself up in darkness and come out white? If He made Himself up out of darkness and the darkness covered Him, then, the God who originated the heavens and the earth is a Black God.[15]

Truly unfortunate, fatuous but understandable! Now, Farrakhan has wholeheartedly accepted blackness as *himself* not only as descriptively defining him and everyone of African descent. What he tried to do in the above quote is to make sure blackness (not people of African descent) is revered as having a divine origin. By admiring blackness as intimately associated with god and origin of things, it is hoped that this can translate into pride in the colored person. Vacuous as it might be, it can console his followers.

During the eighteenth and nineteenth centuries, the origin of 'blackness' became a mystery that necessitated a lot of mythical and scientific explanations. There was the Ham myths and the environmental myths. Some even went as far as to argue that man's natural color is *white* and that *blackness* is a deformity.[16] Well, we can't blame Louis Farrakhan now much, can we? He's not alone in this fatuousness. This obsession with the color of the African Person is amazing and it strikes me as uplifting. Amazing and uplifting because it puts the colored person in the center of dilemma that says so much about the obsessed (racial obsessives, as Adam Lively would have said).[17] The colored person has accepted whatever she's been described to be, whatever its origin was and still is.

However, something has to be understood. Is the Colored African accepting blackness because she's literally black (or close to blackness) or is she accepting blackness for fear of being seen as rejecting herself knowing fully well that 'black' is only a descriptive, destructive and emotively purposive symbolism? I don't know the answer but I can postulate, not answer the question.

There are many negative connotations associated with *blackness* in many cultures (even in my own culture). When a person relates the negatives associated with blackness as a color in *itself* with the blackness of the African people and people of African descent as people described by color black, then a critical view of such associative relationships should be taken with care. There's a part of blackness the Colored African person will accept, but there is also a part of blackness she rejects instantly and categorically. She doesn't give any credible reason for the rejection though. This is perhaps the only sensible reason: "I'm a good human being! I'm not bad!"

Any negative phenomenon associated with blackness is a relative or relation of the African person color-wise. The African Person, and the inherent badness associated with color black are united in blackness. Blackness is therefore the meeting point of the Colored African and Badness (Evilness).

Figure 1

The Colored African and Badness come from their different ways but meet there in blackness (see figure above). Remember they meet only in description not on the substance and content of what they are.[18] When someone says that a *black* cat crossing one's path is a bad luck, then a Colored African person or simply, a colored person reminds herself that she shares something with that bad luck: *blackness*. The African or the colored person might not be a *bad* person *per se*, but she shares something intimately with that bad luck: and that is, *Blackness*.

The branding world and the colored person herself grapple with associating a colored person's blackness with badness by Humean association of ideas.[19] Well, the brander sees the skin as black and knows many bad things described as black (even by the colored person) so he shouldn't be faulted, should he? The Colored African has her mind clouded by the fact that she's black. She always wants to reject blackness but she has no strong bases under which she can reject blackness. History rules; and rules against her always!!

This is what I do know so far. Don't ask me where I knew it from. It is just as true to me as my sense of myself to me; and Harry Frankfurt can argue against my intimately and clearly knowing myself. Call it wishful thinking, if you like. But I'm here to answer you if you ask!

The Colored African had no clear sense of self on a global scale before the branders arrived in Africa. The sense of self the colored person had was very local and intimate. It was defined in terms of tribes or conglomerate of tribes under chieftaincy. Some sections of the Colored African society had some kingdoms which catered for a slightly bigger areas and populations than the conglomerates of tribes. However, the collection of tribes can still be seen as a small portion of what we can now call a nation or a state. Kingdoms were still small and tribally (or largely tribally) defined. When the brander arrived, collective definitions, and sectionalisation of African tribes were requisite for the control of the tribes. Europeanization and alien spiritualization of the Colored African had some effect by aiding the brander in convincing the Colored African that she was a lower human form. Borders and conglomeration of tribes were good for both the control of the Colored Africans humanity wise and for administrative expediency to the imperial powers.

The advance of the brander awakened the Colored African to the realization that all the other tribes she'd previously seen as aliens were actually more or less the same with her. The new person, the brander, *defined* to the Colored African what it means to be different. The brander was different from her a thousand folds. She then developed a sense of kinship with the tribes she'd previously been hostile to. There were many instances in which the brander intensified the hostility among the Colored African tribes to *effectirize* the control of the Colored African knowing the tribes can easily, naturally bond. However, as time went by, the Colored African realized the brander was far more different in every aspect of his life. He was different in intentions, looks and moral outlook; which the Colored African perceived inferior and animal-like.

The brander wanted one thing: to control the Colored African and control her resources. The brander also saw the Colored Africans the same culturally, 'phenotypically' and economically. That made it easy for the brander to lump the Colored Africans up in a very convenient term. This term first confused the Colored African. However, because the Colored African had no unifying term that existed before the brander arrived; the Colored African saw it easy to grab something to hold on to. The physical look was an easy racial consolation. And the colorless person presented a comparative objectness. While the physical look was used as a definition by the brander to put the Colored African down, that is, to lower her in terms of *personhood*, the Colored African embraced the physical definition because she had no choice; or she at least saw something sensible in the description. She was 'black' in color, supposedly, and she was also black by what the brander wanted blackness to mean for the Colored African. Everything she did was black in every interpretation: contextually sensible and positive, and ontically scary and negative. The brander disguised his intentions by professing empirical looks. And many sceptics will have hard time arguing against the brander. The ancient perception of Africanness was then instrumentalized.

She gave birth to black kids, worshiped black magic, and manifested black values. It is hard to really understand the context of the italicized sentence above unless it's well explained. When one says 'black kids,' 'black magic,' and 'black values,' is one talking about these things as related to the African person, or is one talking about these things as being bad? I will let you, the reader, think about their implication.

However, the Colored African tried to evangelize his greatness, which in this case means blackness. What the Colored African didn't realize is that his glorification of blackness is confusing; and at times, emasculating and sissifying. Was she glorifying blackness only because it described her, or was she glorifying blackness because blackness, in *itself,* is good? Or was she glorifying herself and that color was and is not relevant; and that color features only because the brander sings it? The evangelism of goodness of Colored Africanness was nothing but an attempt to hike up a steep, rough hill. The Colored African had to deal with the monstrosity associated with blackness. While blackness was something of uneasiness even to the Colored African herself, she had no choice but to cling to blackness and forge a proud, dignified sense of self out of that vagueness. She rejected every bad thing associated with blackness; trying to present a civilized, decent sense of self out of that sordid blackness.

However, the brander is/was brainy and witty. The Colored African knew that, but the brander has always tried to disguise his contrivance. He led the Colored African through paths that seemed humanely promising. By the time the Colored African realized that the path was meant to destroy her, she found it too late to defend herself. The brander *pre-sets* his ideals and methods of execution of his tasks (whatever they maybe). The Colored African only starts to defend herself from the first time she detects the brander's sinister and pernicious schemes; and by this time, the schemes are entrenched and powerfully affecting.

The brander, knowing that the Colored African was brainy too, used powerful psychological methods that made it easy for the Colored African to look into her own self rather than look at what the brander presents. The Colored African tended not to see a difference between a demonizing description of herself by the brander, and her actual, real se-

If. This is completely an externally forced, critically unfavourable self-analysis. The brain of the Colored African was targeted with fury and horrific might because "the most potent weapon in the hand of the oppressor is the mind of the oppressed."[20]

Once the mind of the Colored African was controlled, a load of nonsense was then fed into her mind. Social, economic and technological might of the brander always overwhelmed the salient, resilient spirit of the Colored African. The weak-hearted of the Colored Africans fell for the tricks of the brander. These weak-hearted Colored Africans started to question their own humanity, sense of self and existential significance. This is the unfavourable critical self-analysis meant for self-disowning and self-denunciation. With the brander saying that whatever is African (black) is abhorrent, the weak-hearted embraced the created, unfounded badness (blackness) of Africanness. The weak-hearted Colored Africans started to dissociate themselves from Africanness which they took to mean *blackness* and *badness*. They didn't delineate the two.

This group didn't find it hard to disown anything African. For example, in Africa, America and Jamaica especially, "The captive Africans were taught that God is White. Eurocentric hermeneutics meant that African religions were of the devil." Once the Colored African internalized this 'truism' it became really hard to hermeneutically convince her or to convince her own self otherwise. Trying to persuade the weak-minded colored persons that Africanness is good in *itself* became a blasphemy because the white god would, presumably, be furious if his antithesis (blackness) is praised. To successfully convince the mentally duped colored person that Africanness and blackness don't mean the same thing was like expecting an egg from a cock. The 'truth' of her supposed inadequacy was overwhelming. And I will save you the agony of wondering why South Sudanese men are soot black and woman are relatively brown. A photo of South Sudanese wedding is a colorful humor. It is made of stripes of dark (men) and brown (ladies). You don't want me to tell you why, do you?

However, not all South Sudanese women bleach. Some are naturally brown. The bleachists (as I will call them here) have no sense of self emanating from inside them. This sense of defeat by the Colored African cemented the sense and feeling of loss of identity that leads to skin bleaching. Constant bombardment of the Colored African with demonization of Africanness (or association of Africanness with badness of blackness) over the years by the branders makes me *pardon* the skin bleachers (or derogatorily, 'bleachists'). And Christopher Charles is right to write that "the interaction of societal institutions from colonialism to the present constructs persistent and consistent negative representations about Blackness in Jamaica embedded in the elevation of Europe over Africa, Whites over Blacks, light skin over dark skin, and foreign over local."[21] The weak-hearted and weak-minded colored persons turned and everything they saw; national and international, spoke of their skin monstrosity, and the inadequacy of their heritage.

2.3 The People and their Color

I'm surprised by the fact that people of African descent have *owned blackness*. They have become so possessive of the color *per se* that I'm always left with either a sense of loss or complete indignation and disappointment. I understand, with humour and passion, the historical loss of sense of self by the colored person, however, I just don't understand why some people are not able to differentiate between who they are and the color the brander has used to irresponsibly and maliciously describe them.

When a Colored African postulates that 'black is beautiful' they mean to say that 'I'm beautiful.' And Steve Biko is one culprit whose position one can see as understandable.[22] However, Biko and company don't explain the connection between their sense of self (their essence, quiddity) and the color *per se*. The two are assumed to mean the same thing. As long as this delineation has not been properly articulated, the 'black is beautiful' phrase becomes either meaningless or abhorrent. Badness of blackness doesn't mean badness of Africanness, I understand. It however, paradoxically, means badness of Africanness by the brander's desires. If the connection between Africanness and blackness is not well explained, then badness of blackness becomes badness of Africanness, confusedly.

There is a big difference between being proud of one's skin, pre-color analysis, and being proud of some identity from without; an identity a person has been given intentionally in hierarchical societies. When a Colored African praises *blackness*, then she has to know that blackness has to be organically and inseparably tied in a meaningful way to her complete being. Just saying that 'black is beautiful' to mean I am beautiful as a Colored African or a Colored African American or a Colored Caribbean is a stupefying expression. It is stupefying to me at least. I will grant to someone thinking that such line of thought is moot. It is however a big self-deception to say that by being proud of color black then one is proud of herself. Even a person of average mental capacity can see a disastrous flaw in this situation. However, I have to admit that when these people say this (black is beautiful), they mean their *skin* pigmentation (whatever the color) not the *black* color in *itself*. Perhaps I'm taking the meaning too literally. Sadly, I'm not and I have reasons to dissent.

A good number of the Colored Africans think that defending *anything* black is the same as defending who they are; which is both sad and pathetic. You have the *Black Panther*, the *Black Power* (symbolized by a big, black fist) and a good movie rating on BET is/was venerated by a number of *black fists*, and finally the *black consciousness* movement in South Africa. It is with this sense of confusion that Fredrickson wonders why evil and badness connote blackness while priests and nuns wear *black*.[23] I don't know what Fredrickson meant to say by this but his question explains the confusion between literal application of blackness and symbolic, metaphorical application. Of course the case of priests and nuns is a natural, inadvertent 'appreciation' of the color and has nothing to do with social situations. It is also good to add that it is not everything black that is bad, but there are a lot of things whose badness is associated with blackness or their badness symbolized by blackness. What I find funny and nauseating is the fact that colored persons try to own blackness in *itself* as consciousness element of phenomenal pride but again, disown all *her* bad paraphernalia.

> **Mid-Thought Pause:** If you want to own blackness wholesome, then try to own her baggage too: bad and good.

When Oprah Winfrey referred to her mansion in California as a *black house*, she believed, with good reason and intention, that she was bolstering her sense of self; a vivid Afrocentrism. When Halle Berry argued on BET '106 & Park' in 2004 that a black cat is not necessarily evil, she thought she was defending who she is: 'a proud black woman'. When a Colored African kid constantly wears black t-shirts, or declares *color black* as her favourite color, she thinks she's being proud of not only her favourite color, but also, herself *in* herself *by* herself. This is even made clearer when 2010 Miss South Africa, Bokang Montjane, and 2011 Miss South Africa representative at Miss Universe in Brazil, answered a question as to what animal, if she was one, she'd have liked to be and why. She sadly said that she'd love to be a *panther* because it was sexy and black like her; a proud black woman. What exactly did she mean? What's the relationship between her blackness and the blackness of the panther? Nothing, absolutely nothing! It is only the sound of the word blackness. But she, like everyone else, is buying into the idea innocently. This is a sorry state of affairs that is real, contemporary but disempowering, emasculating, sissifying.

Hey, colored people, who the heck are you, really?

I might be wrong, but I haven't seen many cultures in which color black is regarded with remarkable admiration. Well, the martial art culture sees that differently[24], but that is trivial to a very high degree. Perhaps it is not any different either because a 'black belt' is meant to be an invincible power or perhaps a killer; still, a darker side of existence.

In my home country (village to be exact) a bad person is called *raan col piɔu*; a black-hearted or a dark-hearted person. If a black cat crosses one's path, it is regarded as a sign of bad luck. When someone dies, among the *Jiëng* people of South Sudan, the bereft people dress in *black* throughout the period of mourning. And a person who's given a *black cow* as dowry regards it, in most cases, as an insult. A white cow (*yar*) is the desired one.

Ok, what am I saying? What I'm saying is that the badness of blackness wasn't an original, idiosyncratic coinage of the Europeans. It is culturally ingrained in many peoples of the world. Anyone who tries to claim that 'black is beautiful' without qualification is making fun of herself, innocently at least. Simply say *I'm beautiful* and it will be up to the branding world to describe the sense of that beauty if it wants. You're simply beautiful. *Black Beauty* is a sorry acceptance of loss and defeat in terms of sense of internal sense of self. Black Beauty makes sense only when we are asked the nature (or more appropriately, the classification) of the beauty we have: Black Beauty, Red Beauty, Yellow Beauty, White Beauty, Green Beauty etc. See figure 3 below.

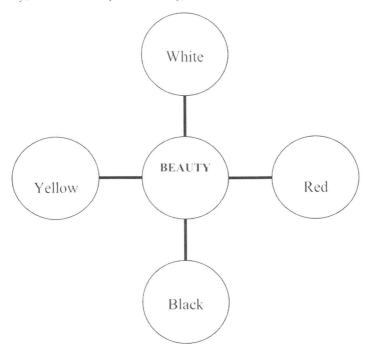

Fig.2. *Beauty Chart* showing descriptive colors and not the color of the people *per se*. The beauty being referred to here is not the beauty of the colors but the beauty of the people 'metaphorized' by the color.

I have to stress that the 'metaphorization' is acceptable if well explained, but it becomes really significant to differentiate between being proud of *yourself* and being proud of the descriptive name you've been imparted with. The *Beauty Chart* above shows us that all colors (as truth-fully and morally described and not as intentionally and immorally described) share equally in beauty and no one, single skin and shape should be centralized and used as a standard of beauty. The only central and centralized idealism is *Beauty* itself.

Apart from the beauty of color black in terms of material things, blackness is socially associated with many things that are unflattering. Well, we all know how beautiful a black Cadillac or BMW is. We know how beautiful a black shirt looks underneath a white suit. These are facts that have no strong social bearing when it comes to the colors of people, except in terms of professional presentability.

However, in relation to human, racially-associated social utility, blackness becomes questionable to own. Night is *black* and many bad things happen at night. An illegal, underground buying and selling of goods is called a *black market*. A day (Monday, Tuesday…etc.) on which many bad things happen is called a *black* Monday, Friday etc. A bad (odd) person among good people is called a *black sheep*. Bad days are called *dark* or *black* days. We can go on and on. The point to take here is that the badness associated with blackness is intrinsic to blackness. Own blackness and you risk, unintentionally and helplessly, owning blackness' intrinsic badness.

However, in Europe and in wild imaginations as George Fredrickson writes, the "devils were sometimes pictured as having dark skins and what may appear to be African features, and the executioners of martyrs were often portrayed as black men." Fredrickson adds that "the symbolic association of blackness with evil and death and whiteness with goodness and purity unquestionably had some effect in predisposing light-skinned people against those with dark skin pigmentation."[25] While Fredrickson presents whiteness and blackness here as being symbolic, their application is taken literally. This has affected the colored person enormously not because of the truth professed, but because of the power of colorless person: *freedom is slavery, war is peace, weakness is strength...*[26] What can't you do if you have **P&P** (Power & Privilege)?

All the girls and boys who bleach their skins are not getting rid of badness of their blackness *simpliciter*. They are getting rid of part of *who they are*; well, externally. And who they are is not blackness as they've assumed it from brander's description. Who they are should be conceptualized and described by them not by the brander. What remains confusing to *me* is whether the bleachists believe their skin is bad whatever color it might be. It may be the case that they just see their skin looking like color black, which they presume 'bad'; and that by bleaching; they are getting rid of that 'badness'. This is something these bleachists will have to answer. These bleachists have centralized, in the Beauty C-hart, an idealized understanding of *Beauty* and not *Beauty* itself. They don't see themselves as sharing in that idealized Beauty; which they assume to be the best. They put some imagined (or externally enforced) conceptualization of beauty in the centre and then try to relate to *it* artificially (chemically).

What I have to say is that people who bleach their skins don't like the way they look. They would still bleach their skins if their skins were red or green; and they believed that something else (a different skin color) was better than their skins; and that they would achieve that desired skin by whatever means. Their sense of self conceptualized by themselves without any external input is nonexistent. Their sense of self is what they've been told. They don't see any difference between who they are and the dreadful, descriptive blackness. If they see that blackness is a dispensable part of them (not through bleaching) but through social reconstruction of who they are, they'd not bleach. Unfortunately, these bleached minds and bodies are lost in the process of self-destruction from within to the outside. I will have to cautiously say that there is *cream bleaching* (losing one self) and *social and intellectual bleaching* (regaining the lost status of the *pre-color, pre-unethical descriptive dehumanization era*).

Blackness *per se* (as applied to human beings) is bad, but people have to know that blackness is not who they are, it is who they have been assumed to be by description. The Colored African people are *not* bad.

Well, some are, individually! They have everything desired of *a* human being; only that they surpass every human being on earth in terms of humility, compassion and forgiveness (well, maybe Vietnamese too). And Booker T. Washington couldn't have put it any better when he said that "I made up my mind, also, that in the end the world must come to respect the Negro for just those virtue for which some people say he is despised, namely because of his patience, his kindliness, and his lack of resentment toward those who do him wrong and injustice".[27] See the relationship between *humility* and *aggression* as illustrated below on 'Civility Line'. Humility would be above the *Civility Line* while aggression would be below the line. *Arrogance* isn't descriptively representative of the attitude of the brander during slavery and colonization.

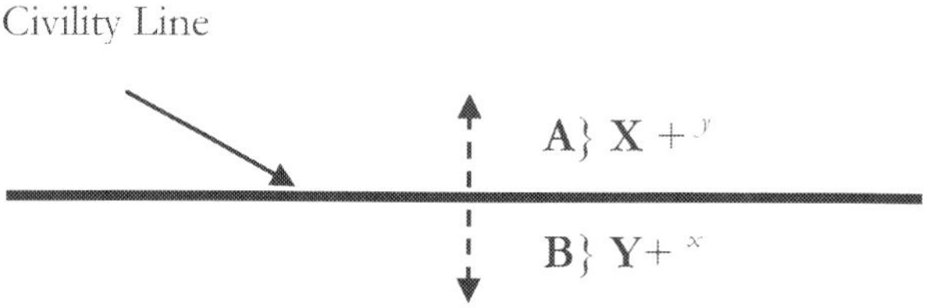

Civility Line

$$A\} \ X +^y$$
$$B\} \ Y +^x$$

Fig.3: *Civility Line* is indicated by the bold, horizontal line. **Y** denotes *vices and bad emotions*. **X** denotes *virtues and good emotions*. **A** and **B** are the *virtuous* and *vicious* people respectively. Qualities of **A** and **B** don't move up and down the line, but the possessors and shedders of qualities do. **A** and **B** can move up (or be interchanged) and down the line but **X** and **Y,** as the defining qualities**,** don't and can't. The ones that move become insignificant and non-defining. I have used the right curly bracket to mean possession of a quality. '**A}** **X**' means **A** has **X**.

Above the line (**Fig.3**) would be all good emotions and virtues, and below would be bad emotions and vices. Note that a bad emotion or vice doesn't necessarily make one uncivilized, however, a sustained application and use of such a vice would qualify or risk qualifying one as uncivilized. Note also that the line can be misleading. Things are not as clear cut as the line purports to indicate. But one thing is clear though; vices and virtues don't move *up* and *down* across the Civility Line. If a person with a vice changes and acquires a virtue, she moves up and crosses the line. The vice she has doesn't change into virtue; she leaves it, largely, behind, below the line. I have to add also that when one moves up and down the Civility Line, it is possible for one to have remnants of vices or virtues. That is the nature of every human being. However, these former qualities are significantly overwhelmed by the transforming qualities and largely negligible.

For instance, see the **Civility Transformer** below for better illustrative explanation:

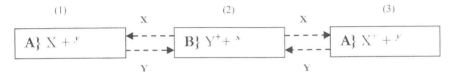

Fig.4. In box (1) in figure.4 above, $x >>> y$; and in box (2) $y >>> x$

When someone changes behavioral dispositions or qualities, they don't necessarily shed all former qualities; they strike an imbalance of the qualities in favor of the number constituting behavioural disposetion. Some colorless persons struggled (and still do) and oscillated up and down the Civility Line. Others remained in their respective sides of the lines. Those who remained above the line and those who moved up the line helped the colored person in her struggle for appreciable and dignified sense of self.

During slavery and colonization of Africa, the European only wanted to put the Colored African down humanity-wise. Calling her *black* wasn't an innocent derivation stemming from empirically observable facts. It was a designed methodology meant to make everything European sublime and desirable. The European centralized his *beauty* on the *Beauty Chart*. The Colored African only saw the European in the middle not *Beauty* in itself. Once the Colored African parted ways with what *is* her own, she became empty sense-of-self-wise and therefore easy to manipulate. The attitude of the colored person and the colorless person can be explained by both the Civility Line and Civility Transformer. Both the virtues and vices were constant interplay in terms of interracial relations. Monstrously wicked colorless people occupied and remained below the Civility Line. They however conceptualized their treatment of the Colored African by presenting their offending vices as virtues. Destruction of the Colored persons' ways and proselytization were presented as civilization of the 'savage'. They euphemized their savagery to sound virtuous. Slavery was presented as ordained by god and supported by the Vatican. Such emotionless savageness can be seen in incidents such as the August 5, 2012 shooting by Racist Wade Michael Page in Oak Creek Sikh's Temple in Wisconsin, USA and the July 12, 2012 mass murder by Danish Racist terrorist, Anders Behring Breivik. These are people who chose or are naturally disposed to be below *Civility Line*.

> **Mid-Thought Pause:** A full container is only useable when emptied. Once the brander saw an empty (Colored African) container he used it.

So when someone tells me that 'black is beautiful,' she has to respectfully sit down with me and explain to me what she means exactly. She should not take it for granted and assume that I understand what she means. She has to help me understand how I can differentiate between blackness as color in itself and blackness as a *fair, ethical* description of the Colored African. The Colored African has to also help me understand why I should dissociate all the unflattering baggage of blackness as a color in itself and blackness as describing the Colored African. I grant that there might be credible, delineating explanations.[28] I just need to understand it to be comfortable with its exposition to other sceptics.

The European wanted blackness to mean what it organically means to the Colored African, not the escapist, sorry contextualization the colored Africans have given it.

First, the Colored African has to establish a sense of self that is divorced from the extending, external valuation in terms of color. A person has to like who she is; skin, physical shape of parts, culture etc. This shouldn't be an acquired attitude triggered by external, coercive social forces. It should come naturally not inspired from without. If a person likes what she sees about herself, what others say of her becomes inconsequential. A sense of self that is not well grounded internally falls prey of marauding, branding external attitude. By the way, the Colored African was an empty container, *name-wise* universally, and the brander grabbed that fact and used it for and against her.

However, the sense of self the colored person has is hundreds of years in the making. Giving a postulate (or even an argument) in a few pages wouldn't make much of a difference. Others would see this book as a *wonder* of a lost soul. A powerful tradition needs more than a few pages to dispel. The originator of the undesired powerful tradition has to have some social epiphany to let go the attitude. I still do believe the world has to hear this word. I'm not ready to dispel anything; and neither is my interest the dispelling of any socially tired misappropriation of empirical facts. My aim is to help people think (about themselves and what they utter) when they utter or maintain positions that are racially motivated; bad or good.

I can disown *blackness* and still be proud of who I am. That, many people will find mind-boggling; however, a good number of people will find it true but socially unhelpful. The latter attitude is perfectly normal, I grant that. Nevertheless, who I am is not tied, by me, to any defined genre of blackness. I am who I am regardless of what others say of me or describe me to be. However, who I am can be compromised when it comes to my interaction with the rest of the world around me. If I have no grounded sense of self, then external definitions or external opinions can penetrate my sense of self and influence my perception of my own self.

I therefore say that blackness has never been good (strictly speaking) and no one should pretend to own it. If you try to own blackness, then you risk owning all her negative baggage. This is a cognitive simplicity. Africans and people of African descent should not think they own blackness. If the Colored African thinks that she's accepted being called black and that her praising blackness isn't an appreciation of the color in itself but an appreciation of her own organic being (Africanness), then all is okay. I would be happy with the just admitted sentiment were it not for the fact that Colored Africans try to decry any demonization of anything *black*. The other ethical connection is the fact that the moral relevance of the African Person being called *black* is from the European's path to self-elevation and African debasement. This the Colored African knows but she is weak in the face of such adversity. She's acepted the status quo wholesome.

When someone claims to like something black, the colored person feels proud. The Colored African feels proud because she thinks someone likes her identity, her skin. *Merde!*

We have to know that someone can hate black things and like the Colored African. Love of *black* things in the name of loving oneself is vapid, vacuous and delusional. Yet, it is understandable why a colored person would take delight in such a preference. What else can she do?

Since blackness was a description meant to tarnish (but assumed a simple empirical fact) the being of the colored person, it is not difficult to disown blackness and still be proud of who the colored person is. The question then becomes: who exactly is the colored person? What defines the colored person? The answer is simple: *whatever you see not whatever you think or want to think!!* A person who is proud of a description procured from *without* lives with a shaky identity. Her identity changes with the change of the attitude of the describer.

2.4 Whiteness

American renowned Author James Baldwin said in 1986 when he was invited as a guest of honor at National Press Club that "white is a state of mind…even a moral choice." And in describing Bernard Shaw, G. K. Chesterton in *Heretics*, ridicules the truth that is ridiculed and the ridiculous that is appreciated. He writes:

> It is undoubtedly true that if a Government official, reporting on the Europeans in Burmah, said, "There are only two thousands pinkish men here" he would be accused of cracking jokes, and kicked out of this post.

This says a lot about how people of European descent perceive themselves. The ludicrous that benefits them is maintained however oxymoronic it is.

I will be brief here because most of the things I've written about blackness are applicable to whiteness; only in the opposite side of town. Colorless America!

Whiteness as a symbol of purity has been owned by the Colorless Europe. Whiteness as a symbol of purity and godliness is claimed by people of European origin with remarkable fervor. When Europeans exalt whiteness, they are implying their greatness. And you wouldn't blame that young Indian man or woman who wants to be 'fair and lovely,' would you? She just wants to share in godliness.

The Colorless American, Colorless African and Colorless European have assumed that whatever goodness there is, is associated with whiteness, which symbolizes their purity as sublime form of humanity; or rather, in some cases, the only humanity. The 'heaven-like' nature of whiteness makes the colorless world step on the podium with arrogance and claim dominion over the world. I wouldn't fault such a colorless person, to say the least. He's simply authenticating his sense of self. While the colored person sprints away from every bad thing related to blackness, the colorless person embraces every good thing symbolized by whiteness. Ugh!

A white color is a symbol of purity and innocence in most cultures. Europeans bought into this idea of purity and tried (for hundreds if not thousands of years) to drum home the thought that Europeanness is inseparable with whiteness. They convinced (with remarkable success) the Colored African that there's absolutely no difference between being *a* European and whiteness. The Colorless European mints no words in saying 'I'm white.' There is so much pride and innocence mixed in that simple sentence. Any person denying this near-naturalized truism is regarded with both pity and understandable hostility. However, a simple inclusion of human nature into the situation excuses the European: a search for a sublime *sense of self*.

Along the path to Europeans' self-elevation, even the fair-skinned Asian is also resigned to the fact that the colorless person originated only in Europe. Even when a fair-skinned Asian qualifies for colorlessness, she fears identifying with whiteness for fear of being seen as cribbing a quality quintessential to the European. You could argue for some modesty in the status-fearing Asian but the Asian struggled and still struggles with her sense of self; especially with the skin, the face, the eyes and the nose.

So when I praise whiteness and say that a white dove is a symbol of peace and love, a colorless European smiles satisfactorily thinking I stamped the 'sublimity' of *his* being and essence (whiteness). A few colorless people, modest ones I should say, might dispute or even reject that assumption; the assumption that praising *whiteness* is the exultation of *The European*. Some will just go with the assumption without any iota of qualm. However, the nature of the colorless European and all people of European descent *is* separable from whiteness. Maybe that is a simple, commonsensical fact that needs no reiterating. It's not that simple, however. Growing up with a strongly inculcated doctrinal assumption is one of the problems against dispelling ill-conceived assumptions.

However, we should not mislead young colorless kids (just like colored kids with *color black*) that by being proud of the *color white*, then they are proud of who they are. These kids can delight in the look of their skin without their associating their skin with whiteness. Whiteness gives them a false sense of significance. This significance should not be sought in whiteness but who they are s*impiciter*. They can feel proud of how their skin looks: pink, orange, purple or otherwise. I don't think any colorless person would feel *low* and disappointed if whiteness is dissociated with their skin and their skin given a different, descriptive color. Well, crazed few would, actually. I do believe the colorless skin is beautiful without it being described white. A colorless person can be a symbol of love, peace and socially 'exemplary paradigm' without his skin being described as white. Delighting in one's skin being described as white is like the same illusion and delusion that had the colored person embrace blackness with remarkable loss, resignation and despair.

So when a workshop facilitator declares that he's privileged and powered (not empowered) because he's white, I sit back and wonder what he means. He's basically saying 'I'm not the same as you and not equal with you." He's supposed to be facilitating 'anti-Racism' and discrimination workshop; however, he's already put himself in a position of power and privilege and that compromises the equality or equity for which he's supposed to be a staunch egalitarian campaigner. You can't claim to be arguing for an equilibrating situation but put yourself above the group you are supposed to be helping reach the equilibrating line. I understand being colorless in the West, practically, gives one power, but when dealing with Racism, such admission is in itself the sentiment of the crowned and anointed 'Racists'; an inclusion into the bad group. And how can I fault a conference participant, who wants to sound liberal and racially inclusive when he voluntary says that he didn't realize that being 'white' is power? And why can't I praise him when he later says that he worked with a group of kids whose skin colors were different but eye color (including his) the same: brown? And how can I fault a young lady who feels that admitting she's been discriminated lowers her status as a member of a privileged group. (She didn't say that but she implied it). Reason being, she's 'white.'

Hey, we are all humans after either protecting or maintaining our *sense of self*. How we manifest this is variable and most of time disguised.

Only a deluded person would dispute the fact that whiteness *in itself* is desirable across cultures. And no one should fault a colorless person for identifying with all the goodness related with whiteness. Also, no one should try to present whiteness as bad because they are afraid that if they praised whiteness, they'd be praising the colorless person. I have seen people who try to explain, miserably and trivially, how whiteness is bad. Racist colored and less informed colored people try to blemish whiteness and instead praise blackness. Well, you can understand why! Naturally speaking, they are deluded.

At my home country, when a *Jieng* man slaughters a *white rooster*, he's not praising the Colorless American or European who've owned whiteness. He's not saying I'm sacrificing this white roaster because Europeans symbolize purity and that Europeans' nature should appease the gods. He's simply acting based on some innocent, organic cultural connotation.

When the Colored African and the Colored Asian bleach their skins[29], the Colorless European smiles and says: "I'm supreme because they want to be like me." I can't dispute this much because there is some element of truth to the claim that skin bleachists want to be like Europeans. However, I have to add that the Colored African who bleaches her skin is truly uncomfortable with her skin pigmentation, however; she's by no means after being European. To claim that these Colored African women would like to be 'white' is both ridiculous and presumptuously innocent.[30] There is no question brown skin is desired by many of the bleachist Colored Africans. I would concede the fact for the colored 'Asian' and the colored Arab people who bleach. Since they already have lighter skin compared to the average Colored African, their desire is to be as lighter as the Colorless European. It is also possible for people to bleach their skins without having a favourable view of Europeanness or without having low self-esteem. It doesn't follow that if you bleach you desire to be a colorless European. Or if you straighten your hair you want to be white.[31]

Besides the assumed desirability of Europeans' physical traits, whiteness (metaphorically I guess) was also desired as a symbol of 'privilege and power'.[32] Colorless people who identify with whiteness define themselves as privileged regardless of what their socioeconomic status is. Privileged colorless folks see the world differently though. Hughey writes that "those marked as 'white'" are placed "as essentially different from and superior to those marked as 'non-white'...."

However, there are times when some whites don't exemplify all the elements of the assumed superiority. To tackle this problem and maintain the essentialist, hegemonic nature of whiteness, the hard-core essentialists fend the problem off by "marginalizing practices of being white that fail to exemplify dominant ideals."[33] This is an effective admission because simple human nature will convince us that the ghost of human nature will always manifest itself in any given human being. By dealing effectively with problems that threaten to compromise the greatness of the colorless person; the sublimity of whiteness remains, in the opinion of hard-core essentialists, unblemished.

As much as some colorless people would want to maintain the historical greatness of whiteness as an inseparable, existential 'Being' of Europe, the realities are changing. In North America now, the colorless person feels lost and suffocated by political correctness. Past historical freedoms and dominance of the colorless North American have been brought to nearly pre-prejudice era; well, in public spheres at least. Of the people interviewed by Hughey, what they articulated is interesting but disturbing sense of self wise. One participant said that "This politically correct nation has become so hostile toward any expression of white pride or even any subtle attempts at whites claiming their rights, that it is a distinctly racist society toward whites."[34] I deplore this suffocation of the colorless person's expression of his sense of self. To be par is good, but to put the colorless person at a loss is abhorrent to any highest degree. Any sound-minded person should not exploit one to uplift the other. The colorless person has a sense of self to be protected not only by the colorless person alone, but also by any *conscientious being*.

The historical dominance of the colorless people; when a *bad* colorless person would say anything he likes, out of *invisibility*, has passed and gone. But this shouldn't be used against the good colorless person. Yes, American contemporary realities are redefining Europeanness (whiteness) and dominance. These new realities should be utilized for the good of all people: colored and colorless. However, I have to caution that the colorless person hasn't lost *all* the power and privilege. There's a lot of unwarranted sentiments among some colorless people.

Another person who's disillusioned with the supposed loss of the colorless place in America says that "poor whites, white trash, whatever you want to call it, they have been corrupted by all the undue excitement of multiculturalism…Whites are clearly victims of this social order. There is always an underclass, you need it, it's functional … but whites are getting sucked in."[35] Never in the history of America did anyone think that such a thing would happen. The colorless person's place in America was as constitutionally enshrined and as unquestionable as the *whiteness* of the *White House*.

When the Colored American was fenced away from the juicy realityes of America, she didn't know that poor Colorless Americans existed; in other words, supposedly, 'inferior whites.' Everyone was over and above the Colored American. When people started to mix and the *undesired* success of the Colored American became a reality of American life, poor colorless people became exposed for better or for worse. Successful Colored Americans started to view poor colorless people with purpose-defeating, unflattering condescension and patronage. This new status of the poor colorless person wasn't an injury only to poor colorless people, but also, to the integrity of colorlessness as a solid unblemished entity. Another person in Hughey's study argues that being white has meant not being able to speak one's mind. This suffocating political correctness has become a daily political reality for colorless politicians and other conscientious officials, who risk losing a lot if they uttered the 'N' Word.[36] Coach Keith Dambrot of Central Michigan University, for example, got fired in April 12, 1993 for using the 'N' word even with the permission of the colored players.

The Colored American and Mexican have the freedom to vomit the acrid contents of their bowels without significant consequences. When a group of whiteness enthusiasts hold a 'white' pride rally in Calgary, Alberta, I see no problem in their action despite their other agendas.[37] Expression of 'white' pride shouldn't be taken to mean 'Racism' because of historical implications. The colorless person should be seen as a human being with feelings and sense of self to protect and uphold as long as they are respectful of others. Instead of ridiculing or trying to prevent the 'white' pride rally, we should support them in expressing their pride in who they are. We are allowed to caution (not angrily confront) them against any bad intentions though.

The sense of colorlessness (invisibility) is either confused or lost. Affirmative action has brought issues that were not previously known by the colorless America. Bad values and indecency came along as the purity of *whiteness* became blemished.[38] This sense of self of colorlesssness is from a group that sees Race mixing troublesome. They want the historical gulf that had divided people of different Races re-enacted to some extent. This group might have some empirical reasons such as *declining* standards of education and *increased* rate of crime in integrated neighbourhoods and schools. However, a lot of things have to be understood. There are so many social and economic factors that play into whether a student does well in school or not. Being in a good school *per se* isn't enough. As one of Hughey's study participants argued, the Colored American was spoilt by both slavery and segregation. "It's important to examine the methods that were used to enslave Africans and bring them here. Look at what was done to the family structure, destroying homes, taking their religion, corrupting their values, the violence in black urban areas."[39] One shouldn't expect students with no credible family and social support to perform very remarkably well as to match the academic status of students who have all the support they need. This discrepancy is something that has to be combated and fixed. And many *good-hearted* Colorless Americans feel it is their duty to fix this problem for better.

However, there is another element of colorless identity that Hughey called 'white debt'[40] or 'empty whiteness.' Young colorless people see themselves empty culturally and they try to get something to make them feel complete; such as befriending Colored Americans and listening to Colored American music. While this might be seen as an honest attempt to be egalitarian, it is an attempt to fend away the demons of the self. To be seen with Colored Americans is presumed by some people as helping the colorless people concerned get rid of the risk of being called Racist; a taboo to a conscientious Colorless American. It is not enough to befriend Colored Americans and readily expect to be seen as a completely welcoming Colorless American. Trying to feel the emptyness in one's soul is not in itself a desire to be egalitarian. It is a protecttive method meant to fend away external bad thoughts and attitudes about one self. While this (white debt) might be seen as a good precedence, it should be checked by the concerned personally and internally so that one doesn't use that fact for its personal significance rather than for the broader view inclusive of inter-racial understanding and coexistence.

In this discussion, what one has to understand is the evolution of the colorless person in the name of whiteness and the sense of identity forged out of it. The average colorless person has been misled into believing a false sense of self, that he owns the world; the "predestined master of this world."[41] This false sense of self is a claim for superiority and sublime magnificence. Scientific, social and technological advances are some of the claims that are used to claim superiority, besides physical beauty. However, this fact only stamps the truth of the achievement presented by an opportunity. It doesn't in itself confer superiority.

If the conditions that allow a given human being to perform a given task are given wholesome and the person fails, then a little of claim for inferiority can be acceptable. Being the first to do something differently isn't necessarily being the best. Doing something no one else has and will never do can warrant being called the best. However, being the first to do something in a given way, and then start to stand in the way of others who want to do the same thing isn't a proof of superiority. It is a show of weakness or protective control. Besides, just because someone has carried an idea to a greater level given a conducive climate, one shouldn't discount the fact that others might, given the same conditions, perform the same tasks.

But this position might sound begrudging to many. As the dynamics of self-identity changes, the sense of self that had been given to the average colorless person becomes challenged in a manner he never thought possible. The sublimity of colorlessness as defining a population of privileged and powerful people has become compromised.

And Obama couldn't have sounded more condescendingly right when he tackled Race issue stirred up by Reverend Jeremiah Wright's incendiary comments about America. While Obama was being the real American patriot, the idealistic approach he's fond of is a food for the knowledge impoverished and needy Americans. Obama writes that "most working- and middle-class white Americans don't feel that they have been particularly privileged by their race. ... They are anxious about their futures, and feel their dreams slipping away; in an era of stagnant wages and global competition, opportunity comes to be seen as a zero-sum game, in which your dreams come at my expense."[42] I don't know why the Colored American can't feel that way too. They can't complain perhaps because of the progress America has seen since the Civil Rights Movement. Oh, Obama's modesty.

However, Obama strikes at the heart of what the average American of personable import would want to hear. What I like so much in the message is not the fact that the message has a unifying overtone for the Americans, but because Obama has a fine political pretension. This is a colored man talking condescendingly right and truthful about the colorless person. Obama's attitude toward middle class and poor colorless America was the attitude of Jim Crow and Civil Rights egalitarian campaigners toward the colored person. When this happens now, you wonder if the colorless person is losing his grip of the world dominance.

A description of *a* people that have been negatively objectified without any possibility of re-evaluation of that negative objectification is destructive to those people's identity and their conceptualization of themselves. This objectification was the name of colored people's game from history to the present (to some extent). Colorless people have not been so much subjected to that negative objectification and that makes Obama's condescending message to Colorless Americans interesting.

Negative objectification of people is an immoral instrumentalization of a human population. Identities change, status quos change and this should be borne in mind. When a colorless person is not enlightenned on how to come to terms with the realities of the changes, then a great disservice is done to such a soul. The colorless person is left with a sense of bitterness and anger, which if not dealt with with great civility, becomes dangerous. It is good to let others acknowledge that a sense of privilege wanes with time; for all people. A sense of loss not well addressed turns into hatred. Colorless people who feel disenfranchised should have their feelings addressed just as Obama did.

I feel for the colorless person who tries to identify or own anything related to whiteness as the way to deal with the challenging worldly realities. Whiteness is good and identifying with it is innocent, affective and understandable. Such identification with whiteness is part of the process leading to self-elevation. Most of the things connected with whiteness are good. What a colorless person has to remember is that, while identifying with whiteness is understandable, she has to know that the goodness of whiteness as a color in itself doesn't translate into the elevation of the colorless person. Priding in a description is like priding in a passing moment only to wonder later on why the moment has passed. A colorless person should be proud of her skin the way it is, not elevate her skin to be proud of that *elevation*.

I would understand insecurities and fear of powerful 'others' that lead people to betray their hidden, frightened inner humanity. Given the history of color-relevance in the Americas, it is understandable why respectable, hard-working men bathed in liberalism would prefer *white* for the name of the nation's most important house. The naming speaks of natural fear and vulnerability connected with dark color in America. While the *legend* of White House naming is there, desire for purity can't be ruled out.[43] And who in the world would paint a house of laws production black? Perhaps a crazy architect would!

To conclude this section, I have to say that both the colorless and the colored people have been misled into adopting senses of selves that are both innocent and affective. However, strong attachments to descriptions, which supposedly define them, become disastrous sometimes. It leads to racial hostility when that description is tempered with in ways the stakeholders find unacceptable.

The good colorless person has been deceived by a bad but a wise colorless person to believe in something he now finds hard to live without: power and privilege. However, a conscientious colorless person has come to realize that the colored person isn't after deposing him from **P&P**. She just wants a mango tree to sit under without being told: *my great^x-dad* owned that shade.

CHAPTER THREE

Racism^R verses Racism^r: Reality and Social Construction of Race

THAT a Chinese man is different from a South Sudanese man or from a German man doesn't need any defending. It is a glaring empirical difference that should be appreciated with ungrudging truthfulness. However, what is disputed is not the fact that racial differences have monstrous manifestations. What is disputed is the use to which Race is put. No one will ever say that there is no physical difference between a *Jieng* man of South Sudan and a Japanese man from Obama, Japan.

However, despite the prominence of all these physical manifestations of racial differences, we have many people doubting that racial differences are real. They doubt that such physical differences warrant people's categorization into different Races because, perhaps, as they believe, such differences can easily be manipulated into a hierarchical structure. As people who live in the age of serious science, we are not going to be satisfied with the simple fact that color and physical features make us different and hence warrant classification. We have men of science who have argued and still argue that Race has no scientific bases. Do they have a case or are they just being condescending to the lowered Races?

In this chapter, however, I argue that racial differences are real. Physical differences give us grounds to categorize people into Races. However, it doesn't give us any ground whatsoever to hierarchize Races into inferior-superior scale. The misuse of Race to stratify humanity into inferior-superior hierarchy gives many (with good reasons) grounds to dismiss the reality of Race altogether. While I understand that Race has been used in the past (mostly by the Europeans) to oppress others, I doubt 'wishing' it away serves any genuine purpose. It only leads to the avoidance of what its misuse engenders rather than the solution leading to the avoidance of its misuse.

3.1 Race as an Empirical Reality

Race is considered

> an arbitrary classification of modern humans…based on any or a combination of various physical characteristics, as skin color, facial form, or eye shape, and now frequently based on such genetic markers as blood groups. (dictionary.com)

I've always tried to see things as they *are* (or should be) not as I'd *want them to be*. What makes such a position hard or at times impossible to maintain is the pretension in which human beings live their lives. A small number of people, if at all there are any, see the world the way *it should be*. However, our lives are not what we decide and do *simpliciter;* our lives are what the world around us forces us to do. People like *Mohandas Karamchan Ghandi*[1] and *Martin Luther King Jr.* tried as much as they could to see the world *as it should be* and maintained their values despite all odds. It would be uncharitable to these great men's historical contributions to conceptualize their works as having been aimed at changing the world into what they wanted it to be. They wanted the world the way it should be: a world that is respectful of other people, peaceful and as *many-in-oneness*. It's possible to say that what they wanted the world to be was what they actually *wanted* and that means the two (what they wanted and what the world should be) mean the same thing. However, what they wanted could change with time and circumstances, but what the world should be shouldn't.

This is a position whose its very naivety makes it highly instrumenttal. When this position; a position of these imminent icons of altruism is applied to Race, a sense of loss of temper and bitterness crops up. There are people who see Race as an empirical categorization of people based on observed physical traits, as quoted above. What makes this position highly plausible is the manifest difference between, say, a Chinese person and a South Sudanese person; a British person and an Indian person etc. Anyone who sees these four peoples will not need any convincing that their differences are appreciably real and concrete. A person who disputes the fact that Race is empirically real has something else in mind. This 'something else' in mind is mostly a safe-guard against the use of Race to discriminate against others. Those who deny existence of Race don't dispute the empirical realities, but they deny Race all together on liberal, egalitarian grounds.

While I understand their position, I do feel they are, to some extent, being patronages, and to some more extent, condescending. And you can see hypocrisy written on the faces of those who purported to be the super-liberals; those who helped in the fight for freedom of the Colored America. These include the likes of Thomas Henry Huxley who said that the average Negro is equal but less superior. This reminds me of George Orwell's dictum in *Animals' Farm* (Shamba La Wanyama): *Wanyama wote wako sawa, lakini wengine wako sawa zaidi*. The dear Thomas Jefferson, despite declaring in Emancipation proclamation that "all men are created equal"; still considered the colored person inferior in reason compared to the colorless person. The revered Abraham Lincoln, in his 1858 Senate race debate in Illinois against Stephen Douglas, argued that even if all Races were to live together, there would still be a position of inferior and superior.

> I will say then that I am not, nor ever have been in favor of bringing about in anyway the social and political equality of the white and black races - that I am not nor ever have been in favor of making voters or jurors of negroes, nor of qualifying them to hold office, nor to intermarry with white people; and I will say in addition to this that there is a physical difference between the white and black races which I believe will forever forbid the two races living together on terms of social and political

equality. And inasmuch as they cannot so live, while they do remain together there must be the position of superior and inferior, and I as much as any other man am in favor of having the superior position assigned to the white race. I say upon this occasion I do not perceive that because the white man is to have the superior position the negro should be denied everything.[2]

To be charitable to Mr. Lincoln, however, what he was actually saying was that even if he wasn't campaigning for absolute equality of colorless and colored folks, he maintained that such a position shouldn't mean colored people should be 'denied everything.' However, what is relevant to our discussion is the superior-inferior dichotomy which Lincoln, Jefferson and others, despite their liberal, egalitarian stance, supported with strong words. President Teddy Roosevelt, who once believed colored and Colorless Americans should be treated on individual merits not Race, wrote in 1905 that "A perfectly stupid race can never rise to a very high place. The Negro, for instance, has been kept down as much by his lack of intellectual development as by anything else."[3] We can say therefore; so much for the progressive president Roosevelt and so much for Obama's intellectual development. Still, President Richard Nixon is claimed to have said that the Colored American is 'genetically inferior.'"[4] And the highly liberal Franklin D. Roosevelt (considered one of the greatest American presidents) snubbed Jesse Owen in 1936 Olympics in Berlin, German.[5] Roosevelt invited colorless athletes but not the colored athletes among whom Owens had won four gold medals. Archie William, another gold medalist with Owens in 1936 Olympics, believed the Nazis treated them better than their fellow Americans did. President Roosevelt didn't give any public recognition to Owens and his fellow colored athletes.

Ironically, the real snub of Owens came from his own president. Even after ticker-tape parades for Owens in New York City and Cleveland, President Franklin D. Roosevelt never publicly acknowledged Owens' record-breaking achievements. Owens was never invited to the White House and never even received a letter of congratulations from the president.[6]

The murderous and genocidal Hitler was 'civil' enough to recognize Owens' sportsmanship with a wave. Okay, let us be realistic here. A sense of self of a person *transcends* everything else even remarkable political achievements. However great the revered men were, they had their senses of selves to grapple with and maintain. Those senses of selves were their loud, negating 'spokesvoices'. The environment one lives in also determines (as per the status quo) one's personal and racial outlook. This tends to shape one's sense of self.[7] The strong-willed are the ones who break with the weight of status quos. Race was a scaring monster!

We don't need physiology or molecular biology to differentiate Races, do we?[8] Frank Miele and Vincent Sarich write in their book, *Race: the reality of human differences*, that any average person or child can classify people into different Races by mere physical appearances. I grant that with all due respect. Simple, innocent Races' differentiations are as commonsensical as the fact that the sun rises from the east every morning. I don't think anyone, seriously, can dispute the fact that *Race* is real. It is not only the average person who relies on commonsense understandding of Race. Even the American legal system relies on commonsense understanding of Race and sees no need for a legal definition.[9] That is simply understandable. However, I don't understand why, strictly speaking, others deny the existence of Race and the essential elements on which it is based. People like Du Bois and Appiah have sought to drum h-ome the 'illusory' and unscientific nature of Race.[10] It might be, as arg-ued earlier, a simple, patronizing modesty or just simply, someone try-ing out his/her intellectual weaponry.

Those who deny Race shy away from the reality of Race because of the *instruments* that have been made out of it: superiority claim, segregation, slavery, Racism, Eugenics, HIV, Third World, World Bank, IMF etc. What they dispute is not what is on the *Race plate* (Arena of Race analysis). It is what gets onto their minds after seeing the *Race plate*.

> **Mid-Thought Pause:** Reality-of-Race deniers are pretentious opportunists, patronizing liberals, ignorant layabouts or Colored intellectuals brandishing their intellective power.

There are extreme positions of people like Franz Boas, who challenged empirical traits by saying that "physical traits could change under new environmental circumstances…"[11] While this is a postulate with scientific import, I'd see that as an extreme, unnecessary evolutionary fact I'll shy away from. These changes in character traits can be considered real too, however, they don't discount the fact that even if traits change, they don't change to make Races physically the same. What Boas wanted to suggest, I take it, is that given different environmental factors in evolutionary time, the known traits of Races might not remain the same and characterization might be affected. Some traits might be lost and others acquired. However, there is a question as to whether a Chinese's environmental changes might help us classify her as an African Sudanese. This seems like a moot point I'll leave for the scientists. Perhaps this environmental change is just impossible. I don't know!

I have to add that Boas was not disputing the reality of physical traits but the misuse of science in categorization and treatment of different Races; a conscientious position we can all agree with. However, we can also agree with Abizadeh who writes that "one cannot simply decide to think Race away in one's daily life when that life is conducted in a social context where Race clearly does exist: falsely supposing that Race is a subjective phenomenon, one might very well, leave the racial status quo intact."[12] I totally agree that Race looks us straight in the face and it'd be unbecoming of us to try to ignore that. Wishing Race away because of historical and negative instrumentalization of it speaks of the staunch belief in the concerned people's determination to fight racial inequalities and Racism, however, it doesn't address and dismiss the fact that physical differences are demonstrably real and should be seen as a sensible ground for racial classification.

3.2 Misuse of Science

Hamilton Craven's article, *What's New in Science and Race since the 1930?* will be very much significant to what I'll discuss in this section. Pride in a sense of self is something no human being should be denied.

Whether you're colored or colorless, pride or shame in one's sense of being is an indispensable part of one's existence.

However, an internalized pride in 'a self' is perceived by people as valueless. Those who regard externalization of pride in a sense of self devise or fabricate methods that allow them to project their sense of being as out-worldly sublime. This type is the group whose sense of self procures a disastrous dynamics regarding inter-racial relations. If their sense of self is challenged, what they do or say in response is, most of the time, problematic if not fatal.

Those who internalize their sense of self present no threat to either others or themselves. However, they are regarded as practically useless, passive and naïve. This latter group doesn't believe their sense of pride is augmented by radical evangelism of sense of self. They hold sacred their sense of self away from the blemishing glare of the devilish, marauding mass. However, the former group doesn't get satisfied with the fact that they are a proud class. They have to have their sense of self known by others. And this knowing of their sense of self by others is transformed from pride, to arrogance and eventually to radical, dogmatic evangelism of the idealized, sublime sense of self.

My main focus here will be the group that tries or had tried to radicalize its sense of self. While the group that is content with its internalized sense of self is the proudest and the most grounded socially, those who externalize their sense of self have a false (or intentionally misleading) belief about who they are. Hamilton Cravens has discussed this remarkably. Cravens derived his analysis from the works of Franz Boas, Alfred Kroeber, Robert Lowie, and Margaret Mead among others.[13]

Boas started to challenge the then held anthropological status quo in the late 1800, however, his work only took effect in the period of 1920s and 1930s when anthropological studies took a different shift. The early 1800s idealism of *Race Essentialism* was put under the microscope. Boas championed the challenge to the historical misuse of scientific information to distort the nature and values of people who were not of European descent. He was prompted by the equivocally informed status quo; which Cravens called 'tides of opinion':

These tides of opinion and interpretation took shape, and influenced American culture and society profoundly. By the 1830s the die was cast. The public discourses of religion, of politics, of economics, and of science all endorsed the notion that the races of mankind were arranged in a hierarchy of superior and inferior tribes or races, with the Americans of "white," or so-called Anglo-Saxon and Teutonic, ancestry clearly astride the apex of the racial pyramid.[14]

Boas, as Cravens explained, challenged such a belief by insisting 'that it was a false conceit that "whites" were more civilized than "nonwhites…"'[15] (See *Civility Line* and *Civility Equations* for *virtues* and *vice* in relation to civilization) He believed that different Races have interacted over many millennia and a claim such as that of European's superiority can't be substantiated or professed with concrete certainty and therefore not warranted. Kroeber, Lowie and Boas mocked the superiority belief, as Cravens explains, maintaining that ethnological phenomena could be understood through the laws of biology, geography, or other natural forces. They argued that what shapes the history of the people are "the habits and institutions that peoples acquired as the consequence of belonging to society. These shaped the social behavior of a tribe, a clan, a people, or a nation. And each such group had its own distinctive history."

Boas continued to challenge the anal of Race Essentialism by arguing that it had no basis in scientific theory and that it was based on "mere, rancid, hateful politics."[16] This position was echoed in 1837 by Hosea Easton in his *Treatise*: "…whatever differences exist, are casual or accidental."[17]

Those who placed Races into hierarchical order purported to have used science to prove the superiority of Europeans and people of European descent. It might have been bad science or pseudo-science but it might also have been 'a science' as per how they understood the facts of their science then. You can't fault a scientific mind for drawing a given conclusion if all the factual evidence available to him points in the way of his conclusion, even when the conclusion is dreadful. So one can then argue that those who professed superiority can't be faulted because they used science at their level and time. If this is the case, then my heart goes to them. It was real science at their time given available resources. Seriously, I have no reason to believe that such a view can be warranted. These 'scientists' misused (not misunderstood) scientific facts: pure and simple. The colored person was coming up world-wide, claiming her rightful position, and it was necessary for her to be kept down through evidentiary juggernaut: Science!

These evolutionary anthropologists (and they unfortunately included my dear Karl Marx, Hegel, etc.) knew the facts but misused them. The misuse of science culminated in eugenics, 'intelligence test', racial segregation and other social ills. The latter view is the position I find both sensible and defensible. As argued earlier, there are those who wanted to externalize their sense of self. A salient or pronounced sense of self that masked or was capable of masking any alien sense of self was admirable and required. And what method can be more powerful than a fact grounded in the *mighty* science; one of the *quartets* we worship in our contemporary epoch. The four most powerful dogmas we revere today are the quartet of *god*, *science*, *capitalism* and *'liberal' democracy*.

Anyone who doubts scientific 'facts' is most of the time regarded with sympathy and disdain rather than being completely hated. After all, it is not everyone who understands the facts and intricate analysis of scientific dynamics. The herd just follows the 'smart'.[18] A person with scientific acumen is the only person who can go head-on with a woman of science.[19] That is why one of Boas' students, Melville Herskovits argued with confidence that "Racial essentialism was obviously a flawed concept without a shred of scientific standing."[20]

Of course one has to have a solid scientific grounding to assert such a radical claim. But time has proven that Boas and his students had the scientific objectivity because their intentions were in line with the essence of science: search for *reliable* truth. Their facts were inside the innermost segment of the *objective circle* (or so I can claim: See Appendix 1).

Race superiority evangelists had their facts in the outer segment of the objective circle. However, they professed that their facts were actually in the core of the *Objective Circle*.

The innerity of status quo busters was well grounded in real science. Those who claimed and professed scientific know-how to categorize

Races selfishly and immorally were at odds with the truth of science but they didn't shy away from interest-leaning interpretation. Misappropriation of science helped this category of sense of self 'misobjectification'. This is what has been termed 'blinding with science.'[21] And it was literally turning inside out.

There is something about those who misused science and those who used it in its objective sphere. The likes of Boas had no reason to elevate their *sense of self* beyond what was required. Boas was comfortable with his sense of self and didn't want misappropriation of science to make himself superior. Those who misused and continue to misuse science, in essence, aren't comfortable with who they are as human beings. They had to grope for something to make them feel good about themselves. While this group used religion in the past for the same reason, it now wanted something that commanded more respect. And nothing did the trick like good old science.

In the following section, we will see how doubt or satisfaction in one's sense of self leads to Racism or Anti-Racism crusaders.

3.3 Fear and Racial Instability

Miss Angola, Leila Lopes, who won Miss Universe 2011 in Credicard Hall in Sao Paulo, Brazil, was asked about Racism and what she said struck a chord with me. Leila beautifully, cleverly and aptly said that "any racist needs to seek help. It's not normal in the 21st century to think in that way." She's right! A stable self seeks no external augmentation of his sense of self. He delights in uplifting of internalized noumenon of grand satisfaction. However, instability of self is manifested by a desperate attempt to radically evangelize an assumed superior sense of self. This latter sense of uncertainty about sense of self is engendered by fear resulting from a less understood sense of personhood. Once a given human being perceives a sense of self to be either superior or inferior, but the realities of the earthly dynamics don't support that assumed position, a sense of wonder and uneasiness starts to settle into such a soul. A soul who'd assumed a position of inferiority keeps wondering about some of the things she does better than the supposed superior, other self. The sense of self that has been internalized conflicts with the ability of the same self. Because this self lacks the means to ground her capability, she remains destabilized by her dichotomous soul. On the other hand, a person who'd assumed a position of superiority gets shocked by the fact that he's not able to do some of the things the supposeed superior soul is supposed to do. To make the matters worse, the sense of self, loss and confusion is engendered by the fact that the supposed inferiors are able to do things the superior can't do. The superior self can't come to terms with the fact that he's either equal to the inferior, or the inferior, in some cases, is even superior to the superior. The superior's assumed sense of self tends to conflict with the realities of his (in) capability.

But because the realities are objectionable due to their conflict with the assumed sense of self, the soul of the assumed superior being becomes even more confused and unstable. The idealized superior 'Existentialist Being' tends to cause instability from within and without and leads to objectionable methods of 'phenomenalizing' and protection of the assumed superior self.

Emergence of supremacist groups, eugenicists, segregationists and all forms of Racist sentimentalism are engendered by such sense of confusion; the conflict of assumed sense of self and the realities of one's social environment. Gilman beautifully writes that "I believe stereotyping is a universal means of coping with anxieties engendered by our inability to control the world."[22] The reality of one's life becomes hard to bear if the possibility of existence of one's incapability wasn't imagined as part of one's sense of self. One has to realize that the colorless person had assumed not only a position of power, but also a position of superior intelligence and $super^{given\ value\ of\ x\ or\ \infty}$-*capability*.

The colorless person realized that, given opportunities and equal treatment, all colored Races could achieve the same level of *acknowledged* intelligence and capacity consequence. Colored Races haven't utilized their intelligence and capacities to a substantive level. Because the colorless person has maximally utilized his intelligence and capacities, he assumes total, exclusive ownership of *intelligence* and *meaningful capacity*. The very idea of such sublimity being compromised or blemished, as per the colorless perception, stirs radical protection of the status quo. Simply postulating a superior sense is practically inadequate to the unstable, colorless selves. There has to be a radical, stern and intimidating enforcement.

Having realized or having come to terms with the internalized realization that one is not superior; it became necessary for the above assumed superiority to be protected, regardless. Something that is inherently powerful needs no protection; however, this group had seen that positions of superiority (despite their real nonexistence) lead to unimaginable level of privilege when assumed. Positions of superiority therefore had to be assumed extant and protected by all 'means necessary'. Supremacists groups know they aren't superior, but they comfort themselves in the very false idea of supremacy. They know that if they were superior, they wouldn't be protecting such a status. Superior status would just be accepted because empirical realities would convince the doubting minds. Because it doesn't exist, supremacy has to be drummed into people's minds; the inferiors' minds. When such drumming doesn't work, the unstable minds become desperate and resort to violence.

CHAPTER FOUR

Contemporary Racism^R (Racehood): A Product of Mentally Disturbed

RACE is a word that stirs a lot of negative emotions in many people around the world. Many have used science, as presented in the last chapter, to discount Race as unnecessary while others have used social similarities among Races to champion the cause against the *necessity* of people categorization. When people identify with a given Race, how they view themselves and how they conceptualize their existence relative to other Races depends on their position in history and how they feel about themselves. When there is deep pride and/or agony in the past then passionate identification with one's Race becomes pronounced.

However, this passionate identification with one's Race takes myriads of paths depending on individuals. While people who have comfortable sense of who they are can pride in their Race without looking down on others, a good many use pride in their Race as *a* crusading doctrine to put others down.

In this chapter, I will present a different conceptualization of *Racism and racism* in order to subject everyone to the old time question of 'Who am I?' While people of European descent have not been subjected to this begrudging question, this book is meant to humble a good number of them into the core of what makes humanity different and good: H-UMILITY!

4.1 Racism Defined

I will use 'Racism' or 'malignant racism' to mean what 'racism' means in our contemporary usage; that is, the use of Race to maliciously discriminate against others. I will use 'racism' or 'benign racism' to mean simple, innocent pride in one's Race.[1]

Mid-Thought Pause (Racism Equation):
racism + radical, fatal, unrealistic and malignant evangelism of racism[2] = Racism

Global Issues defines Racism as "the belief that characteristics and abilities can be attributed to people simply on the basis of their race and that some racial groups are superior to others." This definition will be very relevant to our work in this book.

I have argued in *chapter three* that unrealistically elevated sense of self is a result of instability in the sense of self. I'll apply this view point to people of all Races who're Racists. In 2010, I attended a workshop conducted by *Centre For Race and Culture (CFRAC)* located in Edmonton. The workshop took placed in Coast Plaza Hotel in North East Calgary from November 1-2, 2010. The workshop wasn't only imperative in and for any discussion of Race relations, it alerted me to some of the things I only assumed but didn't think too seriously about. First, let's get a sense of what Racism is. CFRAC facilitators, in their manual had this as one of the various definitions of Racism:

Definition 1: Racism is a belief that one race is superior to another.[3]

I'll stop there. Whatever appears in the manual as part of the definition is irrelevant to my discussion of Racism. The first thing that we have to note is that Racism is a *belief*. I'd want to believe that whoever put down this definition of Race had in mind that beliefs don't *necessarily* require proofs. They are just accepted the way they are. What makes beliefs personally viable is the fact that emotions need something that fits into them like lock and key.[4] Emotions defy, most of the time, any reason. While emotions are, in some cases, satisfied by a reasoned position, our emotions are, in large part, satisfied by what fits into them. If we have beliefs that are established with a reasoned out position, then I'll take those as exceptional beliefs I am yet to find out. The candidates, I think, who'd argue for that position would be *men of gods*.

Beliefs, in my small world, don't need proofs. Beliefs are accepted and professed not blindly but with either cooked-up proofs, misunderstood facts or lame proofs. Whether we like it or not, each and every Race has more or less, a belief that they are superior to other Races. When this is taken as mere belief in whose foundations are found within that given Race, then I see that form of racism as benign and necessary for mental health of people of that Race unless that belief is monstrously externalized to subjugate or oppress other Races.

Now, let me go back to the definition of Racism. And let me go to what'd appear to be a naïve, literal, beginning-of-the-world meaning of racial discrimination. Let's put the belief in superiority of one's Race aside and let's give another *pre-universal-prejudice, pre-color imperativeness* definition of Race. This definition is simple but interesting.

Definition 2: Racism^r (benign racism) is a simple, innocent pride in one's own Race

I know pundits, experts and those who read a lot will find this definition both troubling and innocent on my part. But don't be too hasty or too sure. A sense of self starts with some identification of a 'self.'[5] Anything that is related to that self, once that self has been identified, is then owned. We have seen this ownership with *blackness* and *whiteness*. When the owned sense of self is claimed by others, the response that is produced in responses to that claim of the owned self by another self will depend, as argued above, on whether the belligerent 'selves' internalize or externalize their sense of self. Those who internalize or 'noumenalize' their sense of self will be satisfied with *Definition 2*. They are not fond of evangelizing their sense of self. Phenomenalizing their sense of self, to them, blemishes the very identity they'd want to keep sacred. Their very essence is the mere fact that they pride and take delight in something others have no access to. That 'something' is their 'proud self.' However, those who find noumenalization of sense of self inadequate as a manifestation of a proud self find *definition 2* wanting. "Yes, I'm proud of my Race but others don't know how much I'm proud and how different!!"

Phenomenalists as opposed to Noumenalists (if you'll allow me to be careless here) are troubled by simple pride in a sense of self. They search for ways to let others (whether within or outside their Race) know that there is something special about their Race; that their pride in their Race is not like any simple pride in any Race. This type of Noumenalists find to their chagrin, however, that other Races have the same sentiment of pride in their sense of self. Mahatma Gandhi portrayed this when he realized the Colorless African treated Colored Africans and Indian Africans in the same manner. When he was thrown out of his paid first class seat[6] and later realized that Colored Africans and Indian Africans were regarded in the same manner, he started to elevate Indian sense of self and, unfortunately, wrote to put Colored Africans down as 'children of nature' and 'kaffirs.'[7]

This then creates the problem. To be different and feel superior, Racists then start to exceptionalize their sense of self. When one looks at the treatment of Jews in the twelfth and thirteen century, one realizes that when a group of people threatens the Existentialist Being of a group which has power, a sense of hostility develops. Jews were good in many aspects of life and that made them targets of prejudicial sentiments. Cheikh Anta Diop writes this about the persecution of the Jews in Egypt before the exodus. "The Egyptians took steps to limit the number of births and eliminate male babies, lest the ethnic minority develop into a national danger which, in time of war, might increase enemy ranks."[8] To make the insecure power holders seemingly safe, these Jews were demonized and put down, in other instances, as holders of dubious occupations, or threats to Christendom. This inspired hate and massacre of Jews.[9] Whatever excuses that were used to persecute Jews, one thing was certain about reasons engineered: The intrinsic fear because of the Jewish factor (success). All the factors that were fabricated to kill and expel Jews were meant to mask the real problem: the sense of self of the Christians and anti-Semites. Contrast this with how Colored Africans were regarded by Christians as Saints and Heroes during the same time period. As Jews were being demonized, Colored Africans were being regarded highly.[10] Well, that didn't last long. The Colored African would soon join her Jewish friend in the persecution lounge.

However, this celebration of the Colored African didn't last long enough to be historically talked about as significant. The Colored African was regarded highly then because her 'Existentialist Being' augmented a sense of self of the European Christian. Once the Colored African was perceived as no longer significant to the sense of self of the European, her demonization started with pious brutality

This brings us to *Definition 1*. To make sure what the crying phenolmenalists said surpassed what other Races argued for, these phenomalists started to evangelize their greatness (disguised inadequacy) and portrayed others as either inadequate or evil.

They started to profess, with unwavering vigour, their sense of superiority over other Races. Once other Races tried to follow the same path of exceptionalizing their sense of Racehood with almost the same steely vigour; violent enforcement of exceptionalism started to kick in. What determines whose sense of exceptionalism survives depends on who has power. As long as one Race maintains power, its Racehood's exceptionalism endures. Because the suppressed Races don't always get suppressed forever, the maintenance of exceptionalism of Racehood takes a different turn which is not always desired.

4.2 Racism Instrumentalized

Anup Shah *of Global Issues* writes on their website that "Racism and discrimination have been used as powerful weapons encouraging fear or hatred of others in times of conflict and war, and even during economic downturns."[11] I agree! It's not 'racism' in itself, but its instrumenttality and its marriage to fundamental racial pride. It's how it's been used against other Races.

We *all* hate Racism and we despise people we regard as being Racist even when we do once in a while have Racist/racist feelings. If you've never had racist/Racist feelings, then you're either a big, fat liar, or there's something seriously wrong with you, naturally speaking. However, Racism has become a survival tool, as *Anup Shah* rightly notes. It has been used by powerful groups to further their ideological agendas socially, culturally and economically.[12] What is remarkable to note is how people with dubious agendas tend to use innocent ideologies and radicalize them for sinister purposes. When this radicalization becomes easy to conceptually grab and utilize by the average person of uncertain vision and unstable mind, the ideology itself becomes dangerous. As we've seen in *definition 2*, racism *per se* isn't bad; however, what racism in *itself* means has been lost in contextualization, corruption and instrumentalization of the word-engendered sentiment. Just like other ideologies and devices we use as human beings to make our lives liveable, racism has been used for social, political and economic benefits.

I don't like the idea of associating Racism with power and privilege without any good explanation as to what the connection is. It is with this reason that I reject the following definition of Racism (or conceptualization of Racism) from Dr. Frances Cress Welsing, an African-American behavioral scientist and psychiatrist.

> Racism (White Supremacy) is the local and global power system and dynamic, structured and maintained by persons who classify themselves as white, whether consciously or subconsciously determined, which consists of patterns of perception, logic, symbol formation, thought, speech, action and emotional response, as conducted simultaneously in all areas of people activity (economics, education, entertainment, labor, law, politics, religion, sex and war), for the ultimate purpose of white genetic survival and to prevent white genetic annihilation on planet Earth - a planet upon which the vast majority of people are classified as nonwhite (black, brown, red and yellow) by white skinned people, and all of the nonwhite people are genetically dominant (in terms of skin coloration) compared to the genetic recessive white skin people.[13]

No! 'White Supremacy' (WP) is an attitude (or sense of self) not a system. When used systemically or institutionally, its impressions become systemic or are perceived so. Systemic and Institutional instruments aided by 'White Supremacists" attitudes make the effects of WP disastrous. WP in itself is benign and innocent. People like Welsing are those who argue that Racism is the attitude of the powerful and the privileged *bad* colorless people. This is wrong. Racism^r (as in definition 2) is a simple ideation of sense of self in regard to one's Race. What brings power and privilege (**P&P**) into the idea of racism is the use which **P&P** is put into. I do believe that we can be proud of our Races but still not be Racists. Only racists! However, it is the radicalization of racism that we should lament. A privileged or a powerful person who uses Race to determine who should benefit from his privilege or power has a questionable conceptualization of racism. A privileged or a powerful person who uses his conceptualization of Race to put people of other Races down is on his way to radical application of racism: Racism. A privileged or a powerful person who conspires to kill people of other Races is the very seed of detrimental radicalization of racism.

When some natural and social scientists use science to argue that some Races are inferior and that their existence is detrimental to civilization, then what should be done is to see these people as tired minds submerged in a sea of radicalizing attitudes. This group radicalized its sense of self to the extreme. Their sense of self went from simple conceptualization of individual self to identification with other similar selves, to collective pride of a defined physical group. Pride in this collective group then became radicalized. Race was instrumental in identifying who was to be oppressed, exterminated or used as economical tools. Those who fell within the blanket of that 'proud' collectivism were spared the pangs of *othering* and perceptual *insignificance*. And Sam Harris is on point in *The End of Faith*, when he wrote about religious, excluding collegiality that "Once a person accepts the premises upon which most religious identities are built, the withdrawal of his moral concern from those who do not share these premises follows quite naturally."[14] This perfectly fits racial exclusionary moral considerations. A dogmatized collective belief gains ground with strong, perennial inculcation across generations. Stubborn, persistent indoctrination of the young with well-articulated nonsense transforms that nonsense into truism. **P&P**, when used knowing the ends desired makes racial claims unquestionable social, empirical facts. How a person feels about himself determines how he uses his **P&P** and how he relates to others of different Races.

It is to be noted also that a sense of self doesn't exclude men of *the* gods. As much as we would want to believe that a sense of self to a man of god rests with the man's belief in god, we have to remember that it is the very sense of self and the search to authenticate that *self* that leads men to the idea of gods. To be god's men is to search for eternal rewards; the feel-good sense of self. Once the search intensifies, it brings such men back to the ideal realization that the search is infinitely nonsensical and they are driven back to the very mundane sense of self which tends to awaken the devilish part of them. Having realized the nonsensicality of the search for eternal avoidance of worldly gloom, doom and damnation, they start to own the idea of godliness even when they know it's nonsensical. What the search leads them to is the realization that the assumed godliness engenders perceptual power; from within and without. When the idea of godliness is challenged by any force, the god men start to become hostile to such a challenge. However, these men are wise. They have big, pretentious *books* that help them in their ownership of godliness. They use these books to justify and then authenticate their ownership. Once the idea of ownership of godliness becomes strong, other ideational connections kick in. Innovation and contextualization of the Bible or Koran become apparent as means to safeguard and spread the very conception of ownership of godliness. And by all accounts, it is the very idea of spreading hostility.[15]

However, as time went by and Races started to act, aliens' entrance into this ownership of godliness created a sense of collectivist hostility that is aided by racial identification. We can easily tie this perception to the relationship between the colored person and the colorless person.

Knowledgeable colorless people know that the origin of the idea of *god* and *writing* is with the colored person.[16] However, these two ideas became connected with civilization and intellectual super-humanity and the sense of their ownership became fiercely contested. The idea of god and writing were claimed to have originated with the Greeks and therefore, easily associable with colorless Europe. The fact that they were started by the Colored African was dismissed or ridiculed as wishful or unscientific thinking. Race again became a tool for the struggle for ownership of the origin of *writing* and *god*.[17] All this is done in the search for an authentic sense of self; and as we can see, Race is again instrumentalized for a purpose.

All interest groups, including the supposed men of god started to be hostile to the colored person. The colored person became relegated to the periphery of significance of anything innovative and intellectual. Race was a good tool used to identify boundaries for protection of *invaluable ideas* (origin of god, origin of writing, cradle of humanity etc.) from any claim or denial by the colored person. Once **P&P** became helpful in bringing the fight to an end, Race again became instrumental in making sure that the defeated Races were kept where they were presumed to, or required to, belong.

In our contemporary epoch, arguing that racism is a simple pride in one's sense of self raises horrified eyebrows. It sounds like an idea from a Martian; a pre-language, pre-human-interaction coinage. That stance I understand. Racism[r] now means bigger feelings and wishing of bad things for other Races and wielding of **P&P** by the colorless person towards the colored person.

If a colorless executive with **P&P** hires only his fellow colorless people, then there are a lot of things to be considered. While he might not have any problem with people of colored Races, his simple pride in his Race (racism of a different degree) consciously or subconsciously leads to his or her choosing people of his colorless Race for jobs. He may simply be proud of people who look like him and doesn't necessarily hate folks of other Races. His feeling may just be irrationally and subconsciously conveyed. It is clear here that simple pride (racism), not the radical one (Racism), can too be negative and problematic; not necessarily dangerous.

However, we have to consider how such an executive acted. If the action was subconscious, then he might be excused but still enlightened to address the negativity engendered by his subconscious or internalized, instrumenalized racism. Or he might have done this knowing that his full-pledged pride in his Race actively led to his choosing the colorless people for the jobs while, at the same time, having no ill-feelings towards other Races. Still, his instrumentalization of his racial collectivist feeling might [and at times should] be viewed as negative because it unfairly affects other people's lives. Remember, there's no hate or wishing-down of others (necessarily) here. The executive is only acting out of association with familiar figures.

However, there might be those who act exactly like the colorless executive mentioned above, however, their actions are *actively* intended, not merely internalized sense of pride in one's Race. While our first executive is up to help his or her business (by looking for the most qualified as per his cultural understanding), the latter group is up to promote the presence and significance of their Race. Our executive isn't after promoting his Race. He's only promoting his business in a way he knows better, and in the manner of the culture he was brought up in. I have to add that if a colored person with **P&P** applies the same modalities to either hire people of her colored Race or tries to promote her Race, then the same racist/Racist sentiments can be applied to her.

There are those (like Dr. Welsing) who restrict Racism to mean (not even imply) the attitude of the colorless people with **P&P**. They argue that Racism can't be applied to the attitude of colored people with **P&P** towards the colorless people because no historical or contemporary facts support full-pledged discrimination of the colorless person by the colored person. While the aim here is meant to help the colored person, I see such a perception as empowering Racists rather than disempowering them. Racists with **P&P** would assume that because Racism is linked to **P&P**, they'd not want to *part* with it. Who'd want to part with significance? Racism is therefore seen as a prerogative of the colorless person, especially the ones with **P&P**. Being Racist, in this case, might be seen as giving Racism a position higher in the ladder of significance. If not being Racist brings one down the ladder, then heck, 'I ain't stopping being Racist.' That is what Racists would say!

> **Mid-Thought Pause:** If being Racist takes me higher in the social ladder; why would I part with it? And you know of course that pure capitalists maintain their wealth in spite of some of their immoral decisions. So let me, [the Racist], be!

Should I blame the Racists? No! I should blame the commentators. And I don't blame the young colorless girl in my conference discussion group who refused to accept that she'd ever been discriminated against because, I guess, admitting she'd been discriminated against would bring her into our lower echelons. And that is why whatever is done to colorless people can never be *discrimination* or *Racism* because that would, I suppose, put them on equal status with the 'rest'.[18] A colorless male *can never* be discriminated against: he's the one who discriminates. No one *can* be Racist or racist against him, but he can be! The colored person can only be reverse-racist against him!

As a result, I see the following postulates contemptible, deplorable and *radically* Racist! The arrow (X→Y) shows discriminatory attitude of X towards Y.

Prejudice Equations

> Colorless person of any kind → Colored person of any kind = Racism
> Colored person of any kind → Colorless person of any kind = Reverse-Racism
> Colored person with **P&P** → Colorless person with no **P&P** = Classism

I reject the above equations with utmost spite and disdain. Fundamental, Malignant or Radical Racism is not about **P&P** or being colorless. It is a universal attitude that should be fought off not innocently and unknowingly reinforced. **P&P** become a problem racially when applied to put others down in a life changing manner. In this case, **P&P** becomes contemptible and disastrous to those not endowed with **P&P**. Racism is all about one's sense of self and how it radically relates to other people of other Races. Racism is the operation of the mind effected by destabilizing, affective instruments. How the presence and workings of other Races make a person of a given Race feel gives us an idea of how Racism plays into our lives. A 'white supremacist,' as we know, has no shred of supremacy in his blood. His claim for supremacy is an instrument used to protect his mental workings engendered by the existential prominence of people of other Races. He sees them and feels frightened in all aspects of his life. The sense of disdain he feels towards people of other Races is actually a disguised fear that he might fall into insignificance as a member of former master Race. However, he's wrong. He's wrong that his Race is falling into insignificance; he's wrong about his fear of the colored person, and he's wrong about his elevated sense of self. But he either doesn't want to understand that or he doesn't understand it. I understand it is hard a position to take; that one's prominence is waning.

That thought frightens even the well-informed and well-deposed person of colorlessness. When such a thought (feeling of ostensible fall into inconsequentialism) enters into unstable minds of colorlessness, mental instability starts. If such a mind finds Race less powerful in his fright, he either, in a large scale, evangelizes his position to win racial apologists, or he uses religion; a significant opium of the people,[19] to effectively dimensionalize and phenomenalize his Race Survival Crusade. A supremacist gets mentally disturbed by the thought that his Race might cease to be the power and light of everything. I do know that such a fear is unfounded. However, we should understand how dreadful such a situation sounds: the simple thought that you were the light and envy of the world only to be turned into something insignificant. However, having realized his inadequacy as a simple human being with hopes and dreams made realistic by acknowledging his weaknesses, the supremacist hides his feelings of inadequacy in hate and disdain. Hate especially makes him appear great when he internally feels worthless. The sight of the colored person or the thought of the colored person achieving what the assumed superior person can or can't achieve makes the supremacists crazed.

I have to stress that Fundamental Racism is driven by hatred. Racism^r, **P&P** and Hatred constitute the most deadly form of Racism^R. And this is what marked the lives of African Slaves and African-Americans during Jim Crow, Segregation and Civil Rights; and also the Colored African in the apartheid South Africa.

See Racism Flow Chart for illustration: Appendix 2.

These feelings of inadequacy should not, however, be restricted to supremacists who have no much **P&P**. Those with extensive and conceptually overwhelming **P&P** and still take part in Racism have the same feelings of internal inadequacy. **P&P** parties aren't Racists because they have power; they are Racists because of either 1) how people of other Races make them feel [by mere existentialism]; or 2) how what others say of people of other Races has been subconsciously internalized. While these people have massive **P&P**, their internal men and women are still mere human beings in search of a meaningful sense of self.

Fame and fortune are assumed, pretentiously, to give people with **P&P** complete satisfaction when it comes to sense of self. This assumed satisfaction is only external and separable from their internal personhood. Their internal *person* is still insecure, still searching for a grounded sense of self like everyone else. This internal person hates, contemplates or commits suicide, feels jealous, cries, mourns, lies and tries to secure a niche he's, virtually, already secured. When you see people with **P&P** being Racist, what you should instantly do is *not* to feel sorry for yourself for having been discriminated against by someone with **P&P**. You should just know that these people are internally disturbed. They are internally feeling inadequate. This is fueled by historical indoctrinations (that they are superior) and exacerbated by your negating presence. They see you as a threat, not to their **P&P** but their conceptualized and idealized sense of self. Their sense of self and their wealth and power are not one and the same; they are separate.

> **Mid-Thought Pause:** Wealth is an external fortune of **P&P,** but an internal nothingness valuable to, the disguise of, and protection of, an unstable internal personhood.

However, I have to say this for those who might hold this thought. There might be people who discriminate not because they hate the people they supposedly hate *per se*, but because of lack of understanding of who those discriminated against are. An employer can't hire someone he's never in history seen doing a job he needs someone for. He might not hire someone he historically *perceives* as either weak or violent. While these feelings can still be traced back to sense of self and how the conclusion is arrived at, it is to be acknowledged that these people's feelings are not misguided in terms of the information acquisition. In other words, their internalized affects subconsciously and irrationally grips them. They might be misguided in terms of the truth and the facts surrounding the information they have acquired. We can still urge them to seek advice and get enlightened on some of the misconceptions they have.

However, we have to be careful because emotions, as argued elsewhere in this book, are not always guided by a reasoned position. I can grant that emotions can be swayed by a reasoned position; however, sometimes we impulsively react to situations for which we can't be blamed. However, reactions might be assumed, at a reasonable time, to be affective responses that we have little control over. We can still get rid of these emotions once we get the facts. This is with those who discriminate against others because of fear engendered by emotional responses. These emotional responses are guided by less understood facts which can easily be dispelled.

> **Mid-Thought Pause**: A Racist is a mentally and internally disturbed person guided by hateful thoughts and actions against other Races. A racist is an extremely proud racial person.

To conclude this section, I have to emphasize that Racism is triggered by internal feeling of inadequacy and uncertainty about the (in) consistency of racial relations. Those who are bothered by the uncertainty and (in) consistency of racial relations tend to be Racists if their racist feelings are driven by hatred. Those who are not bothered by uncertainty and inconsistency of racial relations tend to only be racists not Racists. The latter group only prides in the integrity of its Race. It doesn't evangelize this integrity or use it to put others down. This group noumenalizes its greatness in a good way.[20] It is important to add that this group is mentally stable race-relation-wise. The former group not only prides in the integrity of its Race, it takes this pride to another level: exaggerated manifestation. They find simple pride in one's Race inadequate so they devise ways to make sure that others either acknowledge their racial pride, or they intimidate those who don't acknowledge such a pride. This group is, most of the time, mentally unstable.[5]

---

[5] This mental instability is not meant in the medical, psychological manner. It's rather, emotional instability.

CHAPTER FIVE

The 'Nigger' Word: Illusion and Truth

MANY scholars know that the purpose of *any* writing is to help humanity somehow, if not only to elevate one's social status in the community. The word 'Nigger' is an anathema in North America if not the whole world. However, the word is used by people we can call Racists to stir up the emotions of the colored people or people of African descent. As long as they know the word hurts colored people, they continue to use the word as a hot button. However, the users of the 'N' word know that they can easily run to the public and 'apologize'; that is, if they are conscientious enough. I have to add that this is always the case if you are not among the 'privileged' group who can use *nigger* freely.

It is understandable that many colored people get outraged, not only offended, by the use of 'N' word. History can convince anyone who wants to ask why! You can read Richard Wright's *Ethics of Living Jim Crow*, and you can easily see the dehumanizing instruments of 'N' word.[1] While I by no means want the word to be part of our everyday lexicon, I need us to understand that the word is used to make us (Africans) emotionally vulnerable. While I am not going to propose proper means by which the word can be dealt with, I do believe that simply telling people to 'stop' using it or to 'bury' the word is inadequate as the solution. Colored people should start bringing to the fore issues others can talk or complain about not just be negative receivers and consumers of filth others hurl their way. Colored people should stop being intellectual consumers of euro-engineered and euro-purposed intellectualism aimed at making the colored person feel inadequate. We know from history that what powerful people say becomes the truth of the next generation if no enduring countering of such thoughts is availed.

5.1 Diminution of History as a Point of View

What is comforting when it comes to writing history is that it is the point of view, largely, of the one who held power at the time of writing. The writing of the conquered and the weak don't always take center stage unless their voicing helps augment the ego and the benefit of the powerful. This can be seen in George Washington Carver's expert testimony to Congress in 1921 on farmers' request to impose tariffs on peanut imports. At a time when colored people were not regarded in any good light,[2] Craver's humanity was exalted because of the importance of his knowledge to the American farmers.[3] This sentiment can also be seen in how American President Franklin D. Roosevelt didn't deter his wife, Eleanor, whose ideas of social justice, anti-racism, and anti-segregation were seen as radical, socialist and communist by her husband's advisors. FDR allowed his wife to talk against established status quo in order to win the support of the colored population; however, he didn't take any stance publicly to maintain the support of the Colorless America.[4] This is the same instrumentality of the colored person to the powerful.

I call it comforting, to history oppressed folks, because a point of view can never be taken to mean an *absolute truth* even when that point of view might be true sometimes. However much the one who wrote history would want to evangelize the truth in his or her written history, the fact that a person's bias *always* plays into that truth comforts the ones whose history hasn't done justice to. It is also true that history is replete with stereotypes that are "rooted not only in reality, but in myth-making made necessary by our need to control the world."[5] These myths exist even today.

Now, if you have *all* modern day Egyptians claiming ancestral rather than purely descriptive and geographical connection with the ancient Egyptians, then you know history is being abused. If the mainstream historians don't teach students (with emphasis) that Moors helped establish the first modern University in Spain[6], then you know history has been desecrated. If historians don't teach (or ignore) the fact that colorless persons have been enslaves some times in history then you know history is not always objective; and can be instrumentalized for a purpose (Baepler, 1999; Davis, 2003). Baepler's preface to *White Slaves, African Masters: An Anthology of American Barbary Captivity Narratives;* has good explanatory samples. Robert Davis (2003) gives a slightly comprehensive account of whites enslaved in the Maghreb or Barbary as it was also called. Indentured white servants were also slaves in away.

However, a person who's been oppressed by history can delight in the fact that she's been oppressed by falsehood or a possible falsehood. There's nothing as crippling as knowing that history has proven that you've been fixed in a certain niche. If the fabricated empirical data becomes overwhelmingly daunting, the risk of being resigned to the fact that such historical fabrications are true is disastrous to the historically oppressed person and his or her progeny.

However, there is a great naivety and pointlessness in trying to overplay the fact that history is replete with fabrications that need to be corrected.[7] While some facts in history should be fought off with all available might and strength of will, there are some facts whose attempt to correct them fosters their use. The more some facts are known to be emotionally charged and painful to use, the more they become tools for hurting the target groups. If your friends or playmates know you have something that triggers your emotional response, they tend to use it as a hot button. The more one becomes emotional when these facts are used, the more our friends delight in the use of that situation as the trigger condition. This is the case with the 'N' word as discussed below. As long as it hurts the colored person, the colorless person will use it to his emotional satisfaction. Knowing that history can be distorted in favor of the most powerful at the time of writing of given historical 'facts,' one should intellectually ridicule the likes of malicious 'N' word users.

5.2 Necessity of Burying the 'N' word

In 2007, NAACP members, in their annual convention, held a special function to get rid of the 'N' word once and for all. They actually used the word 'Bury'. Detroit former mayor Kwame Malik Kilpatrick declared that "Today we're not just burying the N-word, we're taking it out of our spirit…We gather burying all the things that go with the N-word. We have to bury the 'pimps' and the 'hos' that go with it." He emphatically added: "Die N-word, and we don't want to see you round here no more."[8]

While I don't understand the complexities involved in burying the 'N' word, I do understand the simple facts leading to that event. As I argued earlier in chapter one, the Colored American tried and continue to try today to establish a remarkable, respectable sense of self. The 'N' word was used to put the Colored American down and elevate the colorless person. It was meant to make sure that the Colored American felt useless externally and internally and consequently, be easy to place in the lower echelon of American mainstream. And Hosea Easton put it correctly that "Negro or Nigger, is an opprobrious term, employed to impose upon them as an inferior race, and also to express their deformity of persons."[9] It was also used to degrade the Colored American and to justify all the horrors that were done to the Colored American: *Die nigger!* Richard Wright's visual and emotional painting of everyday experiences of the Colored America in *Ethics of Living Jim Crow*, serves as a good reason to despise the 'N' word. There were lynching, rape and perception of the colored person as an indecent, animal-like person not fit for the Colorless American conceptualized understanding of civilization.[10] The 'N' word was also used as a delineating line regarding the incapability of the Colored American. Randall Kennedy in *Nigger* relates how colorless folks in Mississippi were surprised at the mention of a colored Congressman: "A Nigger Congressman?"[11] Anyone who uses the 'N' word is assumed to be (undermining, justifying or) reminding the Colored American of all those unspeakable horrors. It becomes really easy for one to understand why NAACP would want to 'bury' the 'N' word just as they buried Jim Crow in 1944 in Detroit.

As much as one would want to see this attempt as naïve, one has to look at the history connected with the word and the strength of people's emotions when they address their dislike of the word. The 'N' word makes the Colored American appear thin-skinned.

When the Colored American uses it, or others use it, one has to ask oneself in what context the word is being used. Unless a different meaning of the word comes up, it is hard (not impossible though) to justify the use of the word in our everyday lexicon. If a person comes up with a convincing elaboration of why the name might be honourably utilized in our everyday communication, then I'd be happy to hear that.

What has to be understood, however, is that rappers don't use the 'N' word to degrade themselves or the whole of the colored America. I admit, perhaps 'pimps' and 'hos' contribute, to some extent, to the conceptual degradation of the Colored America. However, these rappers, I think, try to mock the 'coiners' of the word to argue that they can't be bogged down by a description; that that description is superficial and a non-issue when it comes to elevating a sense of self of the Colored American. They believe that by using the word, they are mocking the bad that had been done to the colored person. By using the word, they cleverly gain existential *power* over the 'coiners' of the words; the branders. These rappers are not held emotionally hostage by Colorless Americans who try to use the word to degrade them. They have achieved a level of self-appreciation that the word has become a tool to mock others not to be mocked by using it. This is an intellectually puzzling but incredible collegiality that should be studied. What is destroying Colored America are not the *words* of the rappers, but the way the educated colored people and colored people with **P&P** have abandoned the *colored child*. The gulf the colored people with **P&P** dig between themselves and the *poor colored child* is the monstrous problem. This poor colored child should be educated, not seen as ghetto-minded and incorrigible. She should be educated to break out of the shell the Colorless America has built around the Colored Child; a disenfranchising strait-jacket.

However, I understand where NAACP is coming from and I do understand why they want to 'bury' the word. What I don't understand, however, is why they didn't bury the word 'Black.' While 'Black' is regarded with civility and relative emotional stability, it carries the same connotation the 'N' word carried before the 'N' word was highly instrumentalized by mentally unstable Colorless Americans of the time, and now. People rely so much on the ontic and empirical status of the darker skin as acceptably 'Black.' You can't work inside the house and expect to understand what the house looks like outside without ever venturing outside.

Mid-Thought Pause: 'You ain't *Black*? 'Whatchu talkin' 'bout?'

Note however that explaining the reason why rappers use the 'N' word isn't my justification for our everyday usage of the word. It seems I've contradicted myself given what I've said regarding the understandable rejection of the 'N' word by the mainstream Colored America. Knowing the reasons for the rejection of the word, I have to wait for a well-constructed reason that'd be acceptable to the colored person world-wide. That's why I'm not endorsing the rappers' usage of the word as generally acceptable. However, I do understand the intellectual power and liberating air that comes with rappers' and the colored child's usage of the word. This gives me a reason to think that such an attitude warrants study not outright and ignorant dismissal.

5.3 Illusion of Avoiding the 'N' word

Any person with moral import; someone who thinks he values people as equal human beings, would be careful in relation to how humanely a given group of people is described. A respectable description of *a* people is a sign of ethical civility and moral regard in which one perceives them. If a description of people is done without any thought of moral implications, then a great loss of sense of self is created in that targeted population. A person described without any thought or discretion in ethical and moral consideration is always intended to have no say; whatever that description means to her. However much she wants to raise her voice to complain, the fact that she is of less, perceived significance to the describer, her voice is either ignored or brutally suppressed.

Moral implications of any description of any group of people should be considered by anyone who'd want to consider expunging any negative description or treatment of a group of people. Any description of a human group of people should be run against a well-thought out *moral gauge*. If a description doesn't pass that *moral gauge*, then its use should be checked if not avoidable.

When we run the word Nigger against *any* moral gauge, we find that it fails with remarkable horror. If we run other racial descriptions like Negro or 'Black' against our moral gauge, we'd still find that these descriptions fail the test of moral gauge. However, these purposive descriptions were used *passed* the moral gauge or forced through the moral gauge knowing the end in mind. So, in essence, they also fail the test of our moral gauge just as Nigger does. Negro and 'Black' were not supposed to (or should not have been allowed to) pass moral gauge test; but they were successfully forced through the moral consideration so as to help the describer get away with any moral accountability, if at all he was conscientious. When dealing with people one considers beneath one's humanity consideration, ethics and morality aren't issues that pass one's mind. If they cross one's mind, they are ignored with brutal insincerity.

While the word Nigger was fanciful on the lips of those who derided the person of color in America and other parts of the world, other descriptions were intended for the same purpose even if their utility didn't measure up to the same level of the word Nigger derogatoriness. Negro and Black were ingeniously pushed by or forced through the moral gauge to make them appear as if they'd passed the moral standard that had been set. Looking back at what was discussed in section 2.2, the colored person was intentionally put down (degraded, debased) before the word Nigger was commonly used. The description of Colored Africans as *black*, a word which was associated with darkness, backwardness and evil had nothing (in terms of offensiveness) to do, supposedly, with the word Nigger as socially conceptualized now in America and elsewhere. Well, we all know Nigger and Black mean the same thing only that the former has etymological origin in sisterly languages of Latin origin. It has everything to do with blackness in itself.[12] If Blackness was used to put the Colored Africans down during slavery; that is; to describe them as akin to Satan, then I don't see any reason why anyone would see 'Black' as socially acceptable while the word Nigger isn't. We've already discussed association of blackness with devil in chapter one (1.2). It's just like saying I'm *black* but not *Mweusi*. The assumption is that 'Black' is purely and inoffensively descriptive while Nigger is offensive and hateful. Black has all the negative baggage the word Nigger carries. A colored person is regarded, first, as having no good *intentions* and *value* until she does something acceptably good to be seen in a good light (Fig. 5). A colorless person is first seen as good and well-intentioned before he does something bad (Fig. 6).

I will illustrate this in a diagram below. I will call these diagrams **Valuation** and **Devaluation Lines**.

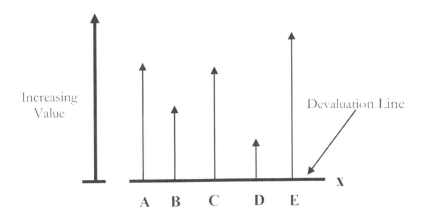

Fig.5. Devaluation Line: A, B, C, D and E are considered bad at the same level until they do something good to be considered valuable or virtuous.

How good they are determines how far they move away from the Devaluation Line. This is how the colored person is viewed by the world. It's remarkable that the revered Gandhi once referred to Colored Africans as 'Kaffirs' inferior to Indians.[13]

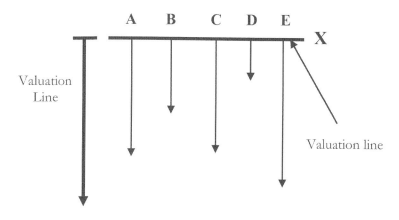

Fig.6. Valuation Line: A, B, C, D and E are considered good at the same level until their actions lower their values and they drop from the *Valuation Line* given the severity of their actions. They are then considered vicious. This is how the colorless person is viewed by the world.

What figures 5 and 6 illustrate is the very essence of Race relations. Figure 6 says that you are good, but if you act for any reason, you either remain on the line as a good person, or you drop to a degree expressive of how bad your action is. The judgment level is arbitrary and depends so much on individual moral agents or the judging society. Some of the actions we do are bad but negligible and so they don't show any significant change that noticeably moves away from the line. (See Civility Transformer) Some people might harbor deadly thoughts but as long as they don't act on them, they remain on the line as 'good' people. Figure 5 says the opposite. You are bad, and if you act for any reason, you either remain on the line as a permanently bad person, or you step into better light. And the degree to which you might be judged as good will depend on either the judging society or the judging moral agent, as a function of your action. I have to add that these **Lines** can be applied to any given social situation and to any give person of any Race. Let me give an example that is not related to Race, I assume.

When Michael Vick was the favorite quarterback, he was regarded in the manner in figure 6.[14] He was good. Well, not by everyone but by his team (Atlanta Falcons) and fans.[15] When it was found out that he was involved in illegal interstate dog fighting enterprise, his value dropped significantly (From Valuation Line) to peak at his badness (Devaluation Line). When he was sentenced and he started to pay his dues to the society, his value started to rise. When and whether his goodness will peak at Valuation Line depends on the judging society and moral agents. It is clear that individuals can move from Valuation Line to Devaluation Line and vice versa depending on the judging moral entity. That is why **A, B, C, D** and **E** are the same on both the *Devaluation* and *Valuation Lines*.

When it comes to Race issues, Nigger, Negro and 'Black' were part of the colored person's branding and devaluation. The Colored African was seen as having no value until she evinced values that couldn't be ignored. Wole Soyinka and Booker T. Washington and others have alerted us to acknowledge the infinite capacity for kindness in the colored person. And I can't help but mention the story of James Bain, who spent 35 years in Jail for a crime he didn't commit but still had no ill-feelings or bitterness for his prosecutors saying they did what they had to do then under the circumstances. The then 19-year-old Bain was convicted (in 1974) of kidnapping and raping a 9-year-old boy in Lake Wales, Florida. John Zarrella of CNN, who talked to Bain after his release, found it hard to believe the man's capacity to forgive. The colorless Europe and North America historically (and to the present) perceived the colored person as having congenitally bad values unless she did something that was considered good, but uncolored-person-like. A colored neighbor is always a source of concern until she proves to be financially worthy, academically valuable and character-wise dependable. Before she shows anything, she's considered 'bad.' The opposite is always assumed for the colorless person.

If any given person wants to therefore get rid of all the devaluation terminologies, they have to explain the difference between 'Black', Negro and the unmentionable Nigger word before they bury one and leave the others. All these dubious devaluating descriptions entail badness and imply the valuelessness and badness of the colored person. Burying one and leaving the rest is a practical illusion. If you prefer *jail*, you might as well know that that is also *prison*.

CHAPTER SIX

The Excusable

6.1 Thoughts Authentication

ANY given, worthy writing should serve a humanely productive purpose. A substantial body of work (scholarly or artistic) should always strive to help humanity increase the distance between our naturalness (animal-like propensities) and the improvement and contextualization of nature's rawness into utility that pushes humanity ahead in all aspects of life. Most works should strive to advance a precocious balance when it comes to description of any human population. And in this regard, I'll put Joseph Conrad to task. He writes, in *The Nigger of Narcissus*, that

> A work that aspires, however humbly, to the condition of art should carry its justification in every line. An art itself may be defined as a single handed attempt to render the highest kind of justice to the visible universe, by bringing to light the truth, manifold and one, underlying its every aspect.[1]

For Conrad, he is an artist and whatever art he produces, will present the world with raw faithfulness: no rationalization, not thinking about it. His artistic exposition isn't exegetical but simple (or complex, face-value) presentation of the "enigmatical spectacle" that "descends within himself."[2] And with brutal honesty, Conrad's artistic portrayal (of Africans) is produced out of the 'terms of appeals' to him as the artist. And for Conrad, the work of the artist should not be 'dependent on wisdom' because it is something that 'endures.' The artist, Conrad writes, "speaks to our capacity for delight and wonder, to the senses of mystery surrounding our lives; our sense of pity, and beauty, and pain, and the latent fellowship with all creation…"[3] I quoted Conrad here because his writing in his preface to the book is interestingly impressionist though loaded with revealing existential lenses through which he regards the African Person. It also presents the justification for Conrad's literary portrayal of the African Person. He's supposedly absolved of any moral indictment in his sordid portrayal of Africans because his artistic presentation is supposed to "appeal to the temperament."[4]

Unfortunately, both the colored and colorless temperaments are appealed to: colored with indignation and the colorless with 'delight and wonder."

But do Conrad's words carry "justification in every line" of his work? Yes, would be Conrad's answer. Besides Conrad's dehumanization (or artistic appeals) of Africans in *The Heart of Darkness*, Conrad's James Wait's (appropriately named) condition was a problem to the safety of the sailors. Wait's health was an obstacle to the sailor's safety, and the impression of solidarity was just but a side patronage. And it's amazing how some commentators try to squeeze out supposedly intended kindness and truism from Conrad's portrayal of Africans in the *Heart of Darkness*. A great literary figure has to be protected from moral indictment. That I understand or should understand! So the grotesque, heartless description of Africans is meant, as it has been claimed by Sir Marti Ewans, to help portray Europeans (such as King Leopold II) as inhuman and monstrous: the core of rottenness in institutionalized European's immorality.[5] How convenient! Put the blame on the certified monster, Leopold! This is a racist absolution of the *intelligent* by the intelligence of the intelligent other in racial collegiality. But this: the supposed humanitarian stance on behalf of the wretched, uncivilized Africans, seems like what King Leopold intended in Congo Free State:

> I insist on the completely Charitable, completely scientific and philanthropic nature of the aim to be achieved. It is not a question of business

proposition; it is a matter of completely spontaneous collaboration between all those who wish to engage introducing civilization in Africa.[6]

Writers should present works that try to help others acknowledge the fact that people are all the same generally speaking, at least, morally speaking.[7]

How some people are treated and their natural dispositions give an impression to restless and tired minds that we have superior human beings. Yes, we might have people with exceptional talents who can pass for limited superiority (in a specific field). Well, they might be dummies in other fields. For instance, consider Alberta Einstein in Dinka Jonglei (Twi) mythologies without any study of such a discipline, or a poor exposure to such mythologies. Differences in terms of individual endowments and inclinations should be seen as the only exception against the claim of human equality.

Those who write to put others down should not be treated with disdain and hate; they should be seen as people with pathological problem that needs our passionate consideration. We should regard people like Joseph Conrad with his *Heart of Darkness* with some cautious sympathy. Tom Regan wrote in his book, *The Case for Animal Rights*, about how Stephan Lochner painted an idealized painting of Saint Jerome in his study area with a 'lion'.[8] Because Lochner hadn't seen any lions in his life, the drawing was just out of his own imagination and was nothing closer to the lions we know of today. Conrad fused the fable he heard in Europe with some empirical 'facts' to describe Africans the way he saw fit.[9] Conrad of course had no consideration for moral civility and accountability because, being a European; he was immune from moral charge. And in the words of Regan, if I can safely use them here, Conrad's portrayal of Africans in the *Heart of Darkness* is 'both understandable and forgivable.'[10] It is understandable because his portrayal of Africa and Africans was how Europe regarded Africa and Africans then: *The Dark Continent*. It is forgivable because of the innocent arrogance inherent in such immoral description of a population. It is with the same line of thought that we should forgive Gandhi on his Racist attitude towards the colored South Africans.[11] Maybe we should disregard such attitudes as

William Henry III wrote that we should not "castigate the leadership cadres of the past for brutalities wholly normal for those times."

A person who is satisfied with the person she is will never try to evangelize her greatness over and above that of others. She can acceptably spread her greatness with careful attention and consideration of humanity of others. This acceptable attitude is supposed to have a quintessential moral overtone. Any claim she makes should be ontologically grounded in acceptable ontic. Rationalization of given empirical facts should be run against an acceptable moral gauge. Failure to do this makes writings dangerously 'mecentered' and morally contemptible. It is with this understanding that I remain ambivalent whether to see Gandhi as an evangelist (externalist) of sense of self, or an internalist satisfied with his sense of self (through nonviolence). Referring to Africans as children of nature who are not used to hard-work[12] explained two things. He had that false superior sense of self (from colorless South Africans) he was fighting against. Double standards! Because Indians were being used by colorless South Africans, he justified work as industriousness to lift them higher than the Colored Africans. It is remarkable how sense of self follows one however significant and higher one is assumed to be. But we have many supposedly liberal minds today.

While Irshad Manji wanted to sound liberal and inclusive in her book, *The Trouble with Islam*, she falls into the same internalized false greatness of self; the attempt to be greater than the Colored African.

> In the main, the Muslims of East Africa treated Africans like *slaves* (italics my emphasis). I remember my father beating Tomasi, our domestic servant, hard enough to raise shiny bruises on his pitch-dark limb. Although I, my two sisters, and mother loved Tomasi, we too could be pummelled if dad caught us tending to his injuries.[13]

From the quote, one can see how Manji wants us to see how far her liberalism goes back to childhood. We can also see how repressive her upbringing was and how grounded she remained to be one of the towering liberal Muslims in the West. However, Manji didn't think well enough about her thoughts towards the Colored Africans. She had to show her position among the Colored Africans, a position that is expressive and reminiscent of "we've never been the same." Ghandi has done that! Manji writes that "We Muslims made dignity difficult for people darker than us."[14] I assume Manji doesn't want to say that dignity is something visual. It is sad to assume that people who work as domestic workers or people who have been subjugated have no dignity just because they are abused. So slaves in the Americas had no dignity? So factory workers being exploited by mindless and heartless capitalists have no dignity. Manji needs to justify her claim. Assumptions of these kinds mask the vibrancy of Manji's liberal pitching.

While I might sound uncharitable to Ms. Manji (whose work should be appreciated), I just don't know whether to understand her presented views as solely her father's attitude toward and against the Colored African (then) or Manji's internalized prejudice. I am drawn to see this as Manji's internalized, subconscious racist attitude because I have no reason to believe she sees her father (then) as a Racist, valueless monster lacking in compassion. Expressing what she portrayed as her father's attitude is an attempt to authenticate her well-intended liberal ideals.

Mid-Thought Pause: If you express the bad related to you, which was expressed against other powerless souls, you're, supposedly, absolved of negativity.

While I understand that a lot of uneasiness might be generated by this book, I do believe that the book calls for appreciable humility. It is common place to see humble people as weak and naïve, however, history has shown that people who are humble have lives and legacies that transcend any myopic claim of 'naivety and weakness of humility'. We should therefore understand the western claim that "we don't negotiate with terrorists!!" However, we have seen the value of humility in people like Steve Biko, Martin Luther King Jr., Nelson Mandela, Jesus Christ, Mohammed, Malcolm X, Buddha and Gandhi (to some extent).

American nationalists decry Obama's call for America's leadership by example. His bowing to Japanese Emperor and UK Queen Elizabeth was seen as taking America to a great *low*. We know America is great in every standard in our time.

Well, maybe not in peace! What I don't understand is how a gesture of humility can blemish America's superiority. It all comes back to what I argued for earlier that while people with **P&P** pretend they are content with their position, internally, they are weak and useless to their inner-persons. This speaks to America's internal vulnerability. It further exposes the fallacy of America's invincibility.

As President Franklin D. Roosevelt once said, great power needs great responsibility. With so much power and influence, the best thing America should do is to exercise its power with great humility. I know realist would frown at this position. They argue for the naturalistic, Kantian view of human life.[15] However, Kant's claim that war and being on a constant state of war comes from our insecurities: protection of our territorial control. We have to remember that a powerful kingdom doesn't worry about weak kingdoms unless the weaker kingdoms are seen to be amassing power that might threaten the powerful kingdom. America is not great because it is aggressive; it is great because it used humility inherent in liberal democracy and *refined, moral* capitalism to exceptionalize the meaning of success.

Security and enduring nature of America wasn't guaranteed by the aggressiveness advocated for by people like Rush Limbaugh and Sean Hannity. America was exceptionalized by unsung qualities that are inherent in liberalism itself. Cheap of all these qualities is HUMILITY inherent in inter-personal relations in general liberal-mindedness. People love America because of the way an individual American is regarded: a person with potentials regardless of Race. And the atmosphere availed to the average American makes it possible for her to exploit her potential to the maximum. That's what engenders greatness. And the liberalism I mean isn't what the average American and European thinks. It's the simple thought that people are treated equal and with respect despite salient differences. My understanding of liberalism would make majority of US and Canadian citizens liberals.

If we are all to sit on the podium, then the methods of going up the podium should cater for the needs of all those involved. If other people are to be excluded from the podium, then a clear, comprehensive sensitization should be presented to help everyone ethically and morally so as to understand the 'whys' of the downs and ups the podium.

6.2 The 'Unmonkey' Business

In the previous section we saw that our thoughts can be beneficial but still regrettable. In this section we will see what is silly. In May of 2008, Mike Norman, of Marietta, Georgia, thought he saw a resemblance between Barack Obama (then a Presidential Candidate) and a cartoon character, Curious George. He made out a t-shirt with the cartoon character and the phrase 'Obama in '08'. The incident stirred protests from a group opposed to his action demanding he stopped selling the t-shirt. Norman refused to budge saying it is something he found interesting and had nothing to do with Race. I don't know what Norman's intentions were; I don't care what they were and I don't mind what they were. Whether he intended the action to reinforce the old-age argument that the Colored African resembles a monkey or he was just being comical, his actions is least of my problems. He can think whatever he wants to think about people of African descent like all the other branders today and in history.

However, I have to say that colored people are the ones who give irresponsible minds and loose hearts like Norman (if he was racist/-Racist) considerable powers. They tend to give nonsensicalities attention and respect they don't deserve. The basis under which Colored Africans and people of African descent dislike the assumed natural resemblance of the monkeys and the Colored Africans is innocent and, to some extent, ignorant. While it is highly idealistic to say that comparing Colored Africans to monkeys should be ignored, it is the most sensible and duly thing to do. Getting emotional when things that don't make sense are either uttered or done is to be both emotionally irrational and irresponsible. The Normans of today should be reminded of, and shown, their own monkeyness: straight hair, smiling lips (or lipless mouth), hairy body, lack of moral sense, etc. If they dismiss their own monkeyness as silly then everyone else should do so. But if they get thin-skinned for being shown their monkeyness, then the next time other people's monkeyness comes to their minds, they'd dismiss it outright knowing their own figurative monkeyness exists and can be exposed.

There are many factors why Colored Africans and people of African descent should not cry foul when they are compared to monkeys. Every created human being on earth has his or her own figurative monkeyness. Let's see why in the next section.

6.3 The 'Unmonkeyness' of the Colored Africanness

That people of African descent always decry being compared to monkeys is silly and it should be treated with excusable disdain. Being thin-skinned for being figuratively called monkeys, gorillas, chimps and so forth, is inexcusable. While the comparison is meant to hurt and stir the sentiment intended by the perpetrators of the monkeyness, it has to be dismissed with *smiles*, and the perpetrators *laughed* at; or shown their own mokeyness. Being compared with monkeys and chimps is neither racist nor Racist. It's an intellectual fatuousness and ignorance; a reason paucity. This is why:

— African hair is kinky and can't be found anywhere among all animals leave alone monkeys whose hair is straight.
— Africans (for example, South Sudanese) have less or no visible body hair unlike monkeys and other animals whose body hair is a protective signature.
— Monkeys have sunk-in noses while Africans have broad, elevated noses.
— Africans have pronounced or bulging lips while monkeys have pulled-in lips (smiling lips).
— No African body products can be used by other humans unlike monkey skin and hair. (Human hair is harvested in parts of Asia and sold in Africa as wigs. That doesn't make those Indians animals, but it does give them their own figurative monkeyness. Caucasian hair can also be used as wigs and that can give them a share in figurative monkeyness)
— Monkeys, gorillas and chimps have no known language or involuntary language learning capacities. Well, we can cite the works of Allen and Beat-

rice Gardner on Chimpanzees and Francine Paterson on gorillas. Koko (gorilla) and Washoe (chimp) were taught sign language but the exercise was rigorously voluntary[16]
— Monkeys have no *well-organized* family structures. Well De Waal might disagree with me.[17]
— African eyes are neither found in monkeys nor can they be found among other animals. Well, some Africans may have monkey eyes depending on who is viewing! Some Caucasians have feline eyes, but that doesn't make them cats.

While monkeyness insults are figurative and not literal, those who get emotional when they are vested with monkeyness should also explain why they think monkeyness affects them. While it is natural to irrationally react to sustained mockery, it is time for the Colored Africans and people of African descent to come to the 21st century. Getting worked-up by issues that are irrational and nonsensical is childish.[18] Africans are not monkeys and chimps and neither are any human beings; not Caucasians, not Asians, not American Indians, not Arabs. FULL STOP! (Well, it would be cool and emotionally therapeutic to call someone (of any race) a chimp when he pisses me off really bad!)

If Colored Africans get offended when compared to monkeys or chimps, then what they have to do is to make a list of similarities between Africanness and monkeyness. They will realize that Africanness has nothing meaningful in common with the monkeys. If it is the darkness of skin, then we have the Japanese snow monkey (Macaca fuscata) whose skin resembles the colorless European, colorless Arabs, colorless Jews, colorless Latinas and Latinos and colorless Asians. However, these people would not get worked-up if compared to a snow monkey because they know they are *not* and will *never* be monkeys. No human being is dressed up in any kind of monkeyness and no human being should be described irresponsibly and immorally. Fans of monkeyness should be reminded of and shown their own figurative monkeyness to test their depths of and the existence of their emotions.

CHAPTER SEVEN

Summary and Conclusion

THE main aim of the book is to help present the case for the nature of the African person, her color, her perception from within and without, and the belief that Racism is simply a corruption and instrumentalization of pride in one's Race. Chapter one presents a personal sense of self in terms of color as described to represent people, and the people in their natural state minus color as described. This is intended to largely drum home the thought that people descriptive colors and who they are as human beings *per se* aren't one and the same. People's dignity and sense of humanity shouldn't be inseparably linked to any given color even when there is natural semblance. Racism has been presented as stemming from human trials to authenticate one's sense of self (Chapter Four).

How a given individual conceptualizes that sense of self once grounded, determines whether or not one would use that sense of self to peacefully appreciate one's existential essence or use it to oppress or look down on others in a significantly hateful manner. While Racist people masquerade as people with special humanity (Race Essentialism) not available to other racial humanities, it is their sense of self that underlies everything they do. It is the same attempt to elevate one's sense of self that leads a person onto the path to putting others down. It is the same attempt to put others down that leads a person to immorally describe people in order to lower their humanity and sense of personhood. When a given population of people is immorally described by people with power and privilege, the weight of such description impresses negatively on such a disadvantaged population to make such population self-hating. (Chapter Two)

The description of the Africans and people of African descent as Negroes, Niggers or Black was aimed at increasing the distance between Africans and Europeans in terms of value of their humanity. This unethical description of the African Person contributed toward elevating a sense of self of the European person. The African Person therefore got lost in the search for a meaningful sense of self to the point of playing into the European requirements. The unethical description of the African person confused the African person so much so that she didn't (and still doesn't) see a difference between her own self *per se*, which is beautiful and admirable, and the color by which she's been described; a color that isn't always beautiful or associated with beauty. Those colored people who bleach have bought into the idea of them being the color *black* itself not merely people described by color black. And that same blackness has been demonically described by the Europeans in anthropology and religion in order to present Africans as resembling demons. Those who bleach are trying to therefore get rid of that badness, the blackness described by the Europeans, through bleaching. This loss of authentic sense of self by defining one's existential essence in terms of external defining attitude gets rid of all the arsenals a colored person could use to fight racial debasement. The colored person is advised to define who she is, not to depend on the definition by external attitude that does no justice to her.

Chapter Three says that despite the fact that many people question the reality of Race because of the way it has been instrumentalized by oppressing Races, it is good to realize that simple physical differences warant classification into difference Races. Even if such a classification is not exhausting, it is intuitive and appealing. Denying the reality of Race based on physical differences begs a question against deniers. Why does simple categorization need scientific authenticity? Those who conscientiously deny the reality of Race aren't necessarily denying the physical differences; they are trying to downplay racial differences because of past historical instrumentalizations of Race for bad causes.

We have argued in *Chapter Five* that while there is authentic truth in trying to avoid or bury the word Nigger, a lot needs to be considered before such an undertaking takes place. When the word is used by others to make sure that the African Person is held hostage by being made emotionally vulnerable, then the attempt to fight the use of the word Nigger becomes a great disservice to the African Race. It is recommended that the time has come for the African Person to rise beyond historical grievances and face the world with authentic pride. It is the best time for the African Person to initiate things the world can talk about instead of just being an emotional consumer of euro-intellective social engineering. The use of words like 'Negro' and 'Black' were also used to put the African Person down. Avoiding the use of the word Nigger without appropriately addressing the ills that come with the words Negro and Black is to be inconsistent and vain.

It has also been discussed that many African people get upset when compared to monkeys or chimps (Chapter Six). This is childish. Whether the insults are figurative or intended to literally hurt the African Person, the comparison should be dismissed as silly and laughed at. All euro-originated social instruments are meant to keep the African Person down and behind. Getting worked-up in monkeyness has been dismissed as nonsensical. It is also good to realize that every human being has his own monkeyness if seen critically. Part of being socially advanced is to be capable of addressing one's emotional vulnerability or volatility without much irrationality. This leads us into the fact that any given literary exposition has to go on its way to help humanity increase its distance between mindless animality and human civility. When works are presented to make sure other parts of humanity are put down, then it should be the duty of every conscientious person to condemn such a work and present it for what it is: immoral.

Anyone who presents blackness as ugly might be right. However, anyone who presents Africanness as ugly isn't. What is beautiful should not be the color but the person in *its self*. Color is only a description and is mostly subjectively perceived. It comes and goes with the describer and his attitude. The person being described remains. In the end, it's the African who is beautiful not 'blackness'; a passing product of prejudicial, belittling attitude. So anyone who says 'black' is beautiful is just lacking arsenals for self-protection, self-preservation and self-elevation. She's intending to innocently say: "I am Beautiful!" Black as a color in *its self* isn't strictly beautiful. No exception should be given even when blackness is used to describe Africans. It's not like there is 'blackness' that is good; the 'blackness' that describes the African Person, and the 'blackness' that is bad; the one that describes some social ills. So Africanness is beautiful; 'blackness' isn't, necessarily. Africans should stop trying to delight in (or be proud of) their descriptions. They should be proud of who they are, not who they have been described to be; and that description wasn't in their best interest.

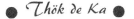

APPENDIX 1

Tzu's pivot (Tao) or Objective Circle or Circle of Objectivity[6]

Most of our problems are engendered by, either our failing to reach the *inner circle* (objective truth), or by our ignoring the facts realized to be inside the *objective circle* if they go against our interests. Most of us, truth-wise, occupy the outer circle. A few we consider *good and wise*, reach the middle circle. There are exceptional people who reach the inner circle. We most of the time don't like these people. They also don't live long enough for us to enjoy their works.

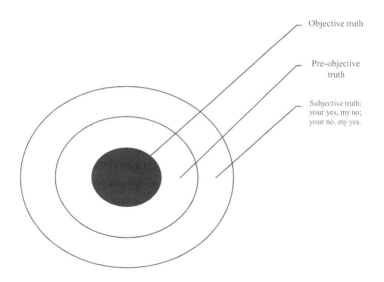

Objective truth

Pre-objective truth

Subjective truth: your yes, my no; your no, my yes.

---

[6] Merton, *the way of Chaung Tzu*, p.43-44. I took this modified concept from Tzu's fascinating poem, *The Pivot* and compared it to my thoughts about objectivity. Also see Regan, *Case for Animal Rights*, p.126

APPENDIX 2

Racism Flow Chart

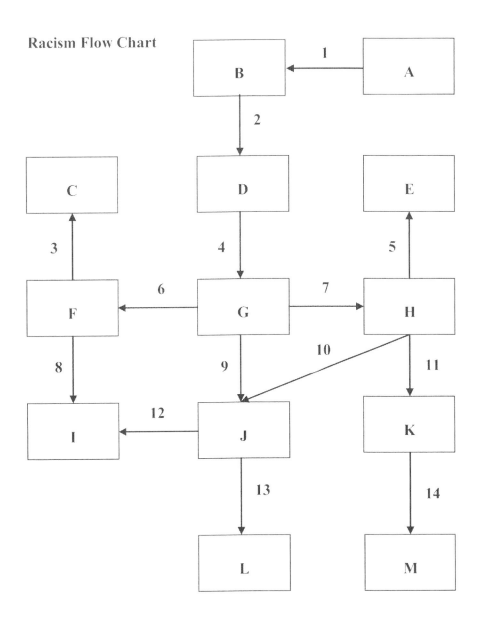

Legend for Racism Flow Chart

Resultant forms of Racism/racism when causal or instigating factors are applied

- A. Human Beings
- B. Individual Identity
- C. Personal Protective Racism
- D. Sense of Self
- E. Individual/Systemic Racism
- F. Institutional Racism
- G. Racism^r
- H. Protective/ Personal Racism
- I. Racial Disenfranchisement/Debasement
- J. Systemic Racism
- K. Globally ineffective/Emotionally Effective Racism
- L. Systemic, Implicit, Grave Oppression
- M. Violent Behavior/Protected Low-Self-esteem or Superior Feelings

Casual or Instigating Factors

1. Individual Names
2. Answering the question 'Who Am I?'
3. No Power, No Wealth
4. Simple Pride in One's Race
5. Power + Wealth+ Hatred (Such as in political offices)
6. Hatred +Wealth (In Corporate World)
7. Hatred from personal insecurities
8. Brandished against other Races while mired in regulations and policies
9. Power + Wealth +Wealth
10. Power + Hatred + Wealth
11. Wield Against other Races
12. Brandished Against other Races
13. Intended against other races
14. When Racists' targets ignore, laugh off slurs

NOTES

Preface

1. James, *Stolen Legacy*, p.7

Chapter One

1. Frankfurt, *On Bullshit*, p.65
2. Frankfurt, p.1
3. Frankfurt, p.67
4. Plato's The Republic, p107 443d-e; Also See Ackrill, *New Aristotle's Reader, Nicomachean Ethics*, pp.377-387
5. This is seen in racists' hearts and minds.
6. Bill Zeller, a very talented computer programmer killed himself after years of trying to fight a sense of self he didn't want; a sense of self that imposed itself on him. The sense of self that eventually led to his suicide was the one that was his 'real' sense of self. He wanted a sense of self that could have helped him live but no, that sense of self was alien to the monstrous sense of self: his 'dark' past.
7. Frankfurt, p.67: Unlike Harry Frankfurt, relative to other things a person encounter, a person judgement about one self is better grounded than judgment about other people or things. That judgment might not be taken to be absolute but it has a relative reliability. I reject Frankfurt's superfluous modesty in relation to self.
8. Daily Mail Reporter, *Black women are less attractive than others'*: Controversial LSE psychologist sparks backlash with his 'scientific' findings <http://www.dailymail.co.uk/news/article-1388313/LSE- psychologist-Satoshi-Kanazawa-claims-black-women-attractive.html> May 18, 2011
9. Frankfurt, p.1
10. Frankfurt, p.63
11. Bandes, *The passion of law*, p.20

12. Technical word referring to the brain's parts and its operatives intellect

13. See W. E. Burghardt Du Bois, *Strivings Of The Negro People, Race and Ethnicity.*

14. Kant, *Basic Writings of Kant*, p.136-137; Also see Fanon's, *Black Skin, White Mask*, p.106; "I am given no chance. I am overdetermined from without. I am the slave not of the 'idea' that others have of me but of my own appearance." p.116. Steve Biko also once wrote that "Freedom is the ability to define oneself with one's possibilities held back not by the power of other people over one but only by one's relationship with God and to the natural surroundings." See Biko and Stubbs, p.92. William Henry has also written in his book *In Defense of Elitism* that "Perhaps it is time to stop thinking of blacks—and having them think of themselves—as a category." William, *In Defense of Elitism*, p.82.

15. Fanon, *Black Skin, White Mask*, p.113-112. Chesterton also puts this beautifully: "It is permissible to present men as monsters if we wish to make the reader jump; and to make the reader jump is always a Christian act. But it is not permission to present men as regarding themselves monsters, or making themselves jump." p.175. Describing the African person is not bad but making her feel worthless is the gravest of all evil devised and put on her.

16. Kennedy, *Nigger: The Strange Career of a Troublesome Word*, p.vx

17. See W. E. Burghardt Du Bois, *Strivings Of The Negro People*, Atlantic Monthly; Also see Jean-Paul Sartre's *Black Orpheus* in *What is Literature and other essay*, p.326-327

18. Allen, p.261-262; Also see Horne, The Deepest South, pp.11, 71 and 99. Crummell et al, *Civilization and Black progress*, p.178; Streissguth, pp.147-160 (Nat Turner's Confession)

19. Crummell et al, *Civilization and Black man progress*, pp.20 &178

20. Horne, *The Deepest South: The United States, Brazil, and the African Slave Trade* p.161

21. Crummell et al, *Civilization and Black man progress*, pp.20 &178

22. Crummell et al, p.11 & p.178; also see Wright, *Ethics of living Jim Crow: An Autobiographical Sketch*, p.40; See Streissguth, p.81

23. Kennedy, p.51
24. Kant, *Basic Writings of Kant*, p.135
25. Charles, *Skin Bleachers' Representations of Skin Color in Jamaica*, p.153
26. Washington, *The Story of the Negro: The Rise of the Race from Slavery*, p.23
27. Fanon, *Black Skin, White Mask*, p.192; also see Gilman, *Difference and Pathology*, p.131
28. Fanon, *Black Skin, White Mask*, p.192
29. Fanon, p.192-193
30. Bigham, *On Jordan's Banks: Emancipation and Its Aftermath in the Ohio River Valley*, pp.86-91
31. *Under Standing Race, civil War, Reconstruction and Jim Crow* <http://www.understandingrace.org/history/gov/civilwar_recon_jimcrow.html>
32. Kennedy, p.51; also see Gildman, p.141: The colored persons place was assumed to be her utility to the civilized colorless person
33. Fanon, *Black Skin, White Mask*, p.132. Fanon writes that "Thus my unreason was countered with reason, my reason with 'real reason."
34. Henry III, *In defense of Elitism*, p.172; Also see Fanon, Black Skin, White Mask, p.132.
35. Henry III, p.173
36. Wade, *Blackness and race mixture: the dynamic of racial identity in Columbia*, p.240 & p.378
37. Bederman, *Manliness & Civilization*, p.58
38. Solnit, *Reconstructing the Strong of Hurricane Katarina at Five, Nation*, pp.11-12
39. See Solnit's article in the Nation
40. See Solnit's article in the Nation
41. See Solnit article in the Nation; Also see Charles, *Skin Bleachers' Representations of Skin Color in Jamaica*, p.158. The African American heroes who helped during Hurricane Katarina were either ignored or portrayed in bad life. This is the same Thing Charles says in about Colored heroes in Jamaica.
42. Henry III, *In defense of Elitism*, P.173

43. See Peter Singer's *Morality, Reasons and the Right of Animals*, in De Waal's *Primates and Philosophers*, p.140-158.Briley, *Cry Freedom*, p.11
44. Briley, *Cry Freedom*, p.11. This brutal (and required) honesty is matched by William Henry III when he wrote against the claim that ancient Egyptian civilization was a black civilization. Henry III writes that: "Quiet apart from the thinness, to put it politely, of evidence supporting this claim, the problem is how to explain the almost total lack of progress in science, technology, hygiene, and medicine among later African peoples. If they had such a great head start, what does it say about their culture that is all drifted away?" Henry III, *In Defense of Elitism*, p.45. This is the explanation that Biko (and any honest African) honestly conceded or should concede.
45. Harris, *End of Faith*, p.175
46. Harris, p.175
47. Sartre, *Anti-Semite and Jew*, p.95
48. Anthony Lambede as quoted by Nelson Mandela in his memoir, *Long Work to Freedom*p.
49. Christophe Konkobo, *Dark Continent, Dark Stage Body Performance in Colonial. Theatre and Cinema*, p.1094
50. Horvitz et al, *Encyclopedia of War Crimes and Genocide*, p.227
51. See Biko's quotations on South African History Online: "The most potent weapon in the hand of the oppressor is the mind of the oppressed." Also see Biko and Stubb, p.29
52. Fanon, *Black Skin White Mask*, p.109
53. See Biko's quotations on South African History Online
54. Maimonides, *The Guide of the Perplexed*, p.280
55. Fanon, *Black Skin, White Mask*, p.113
56. Prunier, *Africa's World War: Congo, The Rwandan genocide and the making of a Continental Catastrophe*, p.xxix
57. See Biko and Stubbs, *I like what I write*: selected writings, pp. 68 & 92See Biko's quotations on South African History Online
58. Wole Soyinka, *Nobel Lecture*, Nobelprize.org. 4 Feb 2011
59. See note 58 above

60. Orangeburg Massacre: survivors tell their stories (video), <http://withintheblackcommunity.blogspot.com>. Orangeburg Massacre of February 8, 1968 is a testimony of how the colored person attempt to entrench a decent, credible sense of self in America was fought with furor, fury and horror. The forces who were supposed to protect the people killed the follow students: Samuel Hammond Jr., Delano Middleton and Henry Smith. The simple thought of the colored student achieving the same status 'immoralized' South Carolina High Way patrollers.
61. See Cheikh Anta Diop's *African Origin or Civilization*; also See Franz Fanon's quote of Victor Schoelcher's book, *Slavery and Colonization*, p.130-132

Chapter Two

1. Fredrickson, *Racism: a short history*, pp.26-28
2. Fredrickson, *Racism: a brief history*, pp.26-28
3. Keim, *Mistaking Africa*, p.28
4. Keim, p.28
5. See *Slavery*, edited by Thomas Streissguth, p.10
6. Allen, *The Invention of White Race, the origin of racial oppression in Anglo-America*, p.8
7. Allen, p.8, pp.36-42
8. Allen, 8, pp.36-42
9. Russell, *Why I'm not a Christian*, p.26; also see Dawkin, *The God Delusion*, p.314. Dawkins writes that "Pope Pius XII's persistent refusal to take a stand against the Nazis—a subject of considerable embarrassment to the modern Church." This is an express manifestation of how the Church in history contributed towards the oppression of the *oppressed* groups.
10. Soyinka writes that "There is a deep lesson for the world in the black races' capacity to forgive, one which, I often think, has much to do with ethical precepts which spring from their world view and authentic religions, none of which is ever totally eradicated by the accretions of foreign faiths and their implicit

ethnocentricism." See "Wole Soyinka - Nobel Lecture". Nobelprize.org. 4 Feb 2011 http://nobelprize.org/nobel_prizes/literature/laureates/1986/soyinka-lecture.html. Also see Booker T. Washington, *The Story of the Negro*, p.12

11. Sons of Noah
12. Fredrickson, *Racism: a brief history*, p.29
13. Wade, *Blackness and Race mixture: dynamics of racial identity in Columbia*, p.240
14. See Biko's Writings on South African history Online
15. Farrakhan, Louis, *The Origin of Blackness*, delivered at Mosque Maryam Chicago on April 8, 2001.
16. Lively, *Masks: blackness, race, and the imagination*, p.28
17. Lively, p.37
18. Remember the brander wanted blackness to mean both the description and badness for the Colored African. So the application of blackness to the Colored African by the branding Europe wasn't innocent or unintentional.
19. Hume, *Inquiry Concerning Human Understanding*, p.14
20. See Biko's Writings on South African history Online
21. Charless, p.162; Also see Algambi, p.1216
22. Biko and Stubbs, *I like what I write*, p.48
23. Fredrickson, *Racism; a brief history*, p.26
24. See The Black Martial Art Academy website. The highest belt is given to the best martial art rank. http://www.blacksmartialartsacademy.com/academy.html; also see Thomas William, *Why is it the most popular weapon in Martial arts*, The Black Belt, April 1997, 35-37, pp.96-99. Famous black belt holders are Chuck Norris, Cynthia Rothrock, Jackie Chan, among others
25. Fredrickson, *Racism: a brief history*, p.26
26. Orwell, *Nineteen Eighty-Four*, p
27. Washington, *The Story of the Negro*, p.12

28. Perhaps there is that good blackness which describes the Colored African and that bad blackness that doesn't describe here. The question is, true as that might be, how do we make sense of that?
29. See Algambi's Article on *Skin Bleaching in Saudi Arabia*
30. Hall, *The Bleaching Syndrome in the Context of Somatic Norm Image Among Women of Color: A Qualitative Analysis of Skin Color Bleaching Syndrome, Somatic Norm Image and Women of Color*, p.180
31. See Mariame Kaba's article on http://www.donnamagazine.info/mariamefive.html
32. Hughey, p.1291
33. Hughey, p.1292
34. Hughey, p.1295
35. Hughey, p.1295
36. Kennedy, pp.8 & 12
37. See Calgary Herald's article
38. Hughey, pp.1297-1299
39. Hughey, p.1298
40. Hughey, p.1299
41. Fanon, *Black Skin, White Mask*, p.129
42. Andrew Malcolm, *Barack Obama tackles race in Philadelphia speech*, Los Angeles Times, March 18, 2008.
43. Seale, *The President's House, A History*. Volume I, pp. 1, 23.

Chapter Three

1. Well, we can disregard his attitude towards the Colored African in South Africa. Some people called him Racist because of his false

sense of superiority towards Colored Africans. He was only manifesting his sense of self as any normal human being would.
2. See collected works of Abraham Lincoln. Also see Dawkins' *The God Delusion*, p.302. You can find both Huxley's and Lincoln's quotes of their 'Zeitgeistic' view on Negro.
3. Miele and Sarich, *Race: The reality of race difference*, p.2
4. Miele and Sarich, p.2
5. Schaap, *Triumph: the untold story of Jesse Owens and Hitler's Olympics*, p.211
6. See Jesse Owens and the 1936 Berlin Olympics. Also see William Henry III's *In Defense of Elitism*, p.80. Asked about the way German Nazis treated them (black athletes), Williams cynically said: "Well, at least they didn't ask us to ride at the back of the bus."
7. See Steger, *Gandi's Dilemma*, p.61. We should see both Gandhi and Roosevelt not necessarily Racists, but people coerced by their senses of selves reinforced by the status quo. It was natural for the Africans and American-Americans to be viewed in the manner the two men perceived them. It was right by their time and standard. What I have to caution you about is the nature of inner 'spokesvoices' of every person; tending to one's existential essence: sense of self. I have to remind you of the unfortunate fact that we only seem to excuse the bad by citing the standard mores or Zeitgeists of the time when it comes to *bad* deeds. This is not applied to good deeds. Good deeds are subjected to any zeitgeist. See Dawkins, *The God Delusion*, pp.298-308. Also see William Henry III argument that "It is typical of the hostile, aggrieved posture of multiculturalists to discredit men who were virtuous by the mores of their times through the retroactive imposition of today's values and beliefs." William, p.90
8. Miele and Sarich, Race: *The reality of race difference*, p.3
9. Miele and Sarich, p.14
10. See Appiah's Chapter Two in *In My Father's House*; Also see Du Bois, *Dusk of Dawn: An Essay Toward an Autobiography of a Race Concept*, p.137

11. Craven, *What's New in Science and Race since the 1930?: Anthropologists and Racial Essentialism*, p.304
12. Arash Abizadeh, Ethnicity, Race, And A Possible Humanity, p. 27
13. Cravens, p.301
14. Cravens, p.300
15. Cravens, p.302
16. Cravens, p.302; also see Cashmore and Jennings, p. xiv & p.10
17. Easton, *Treatise on the Intellectual Character and Civil and Political Condition of the Colored people of the United States: and the Prejudice Exercised Towards Them*, p.5
18. Marcus, *The Sentimental Citizen*, pp.101-1-3
19. And you can't argue with Mark Hocutt when he writes in his review of a book by Frank Miele and Vincent Sarich: *The Reality of Human Differences*. He writes that "The authors bring impressive credentials to their work. Sarich, a retired professor of anthropology, was one of the pioneers in using molecular biology to understand human origins. Miele, an editor of Skeptic magazine, has made a career of interviewing distinguished scientists and writing lucid accounts of their work for the general public." See Hocutt's Review of *The Reality of Human Difference* <http://metapsychology.mentalhelp.net/poc/view_doc.php?type=book&id=2085>; Also see Acrill's *New Aristotle Reader*, p.364 (1095a); Aristotle explains the credibility of judgment as rooted in knowledge. A person who lacks knowledge is a field will not be a 'good judge.'
20. Cravens, p.304
21. Dawkins, *The God Delusion*, p.109: The great and religious mathematician Euler challenged an atheist, Diderot, that god exists and gave the following equation: $(a + b^n)/n = x$. If one doesn't know or doesn't understand what the equation says, then one is likely to appear convinced if not lost.
22. Gilman, *Difference and Pathology*, p.12

Chapter Four

1. While this differentiation might appear unparsimonious, I see it necessary for understanding the very idea of Racism and how to combat it.
2. Racism' will have lower case (r)superscript after it if it appears at the beginning of the sentence to differentiate it from Racism.
3. Centre for Race and Culture Manual; see also Gilman, *Difference and Pathology*, p.141 and also see Skidmore, Black into White, p.64, 65
4. Garang, Kuir ë, *Myths and Incapacities; glorification of human weakness*, unpublished manuscript
5. This is extensively discussed in *Myths and Incapacities*. Also see Chersterton, *Heretics*, p.122
6. Nojeim, *Gandhi and King*, p.73-74
7. Steger, p.61
8. Diop, *African Origin of Civilization*, p. 7
9. Fredrickson, *Racism; a short history*, p.19 & 21-23
10. Fredrickson, *Racism; a brief history*, p.27-28
11. See Anub Shah's article on Global Issues website.
12. Cashmore and Jennings, *Racism: Essential Readings*, p.xiii; Skidmore, *Black into White*, p.70, p.116 & 117
13. See Dr. Frances Cress Welsing's quote on http://www.africawithin.com/welsing/welsing.htm
14. Harris, *End of Faith*, p.177
15. Note that I do believe that religion; the good one that is, is a necessary part of our contemporary society. What I abhor is what is purported to be religion when it is actually me-centered myopia.
16. Ben-Jochannan, *The black Man of the Nile*, p.xx, p.xxi, p.316, p.382; Also see Yosef Ben-Jochannan, Speech at Tuskegee. *The Black Man Must Wake up* <http://themilwaukeedrum.com/2010/10/13/dr-yosef-ben-jochannan-video-the-black-man-must-wake-up/>

17. Ben-Jochannan, *The Black Man of the Nile*, p.xx, p.xxi, p.316, p.382
18. Singer, *Practical Ethics*, p.48
19. Marx, *Critique of Hegel's 'philosophy of Right'* p.131; Also see Neitztsche, *Beyond God and Evil*, p.73. "...gave comfort to sufferers, courage to the oppressed and despairing..." p.75
20. There are those who noumenalize badness and there are those who phenomenalize badness. There are also those who noumenalized goodness and there are also those who phenomenalize goodness. We should take noumenalization to
21. be good and phenomenalization to be bad. They can go either way.

Chapter Five

1. Wright, *Ethics of Living Jim Crow*, 1937
2. Freedman, *Eleanor Roosevelt: A Life of Discovery*, p.110
3. McMurry, George Washington Carver: Scientist and Symbol, p.174
4. Freeman, p.109
5. Gilman, *Difference and Pathology, stereotype of sexuality, race and madness*, p.12
6. See Ben-Jochannan's Lecture at Tuskegee
7. Maybe that is what I am doing in this book.
8. Joel Roberts, *Burying The N-Word; NAACP Symbolically Buries Racist Word During Public Ceremony In Detroit*, July 09, 2007 http://www.cbsnews.com/stories/2007/07/09/national/main3032635.shtml
9. Easton, p.40
10. Wright, *Ethics of Living Jim Crow*, p.42
11. Kennedy, p.46
12. Kennedy, p.4
13. Steger, *Gandhi's Dilemma: nonviolent principles and nationalist power*, p.61
14. See Allan Judd article in The Altanta Journal-Constitution
15. See Judd's article on Michael Vick

Chapter Six

1. Conrad, *The Niger of Narcissus*, p.i
2. Conrad, p.ii
3. Conrad, p.iii
4. Conrad, p.iv
5. Ewans, *European Atrocity, African Catastrophe*, pp.4 &5
6. Ewans, p.40
7. Regan, *The Case for Animal rights*, pp.233-239
8. Regan, pp.1-2. Also see Chesterton's *Heretics*, p.174
9. Gilman, p.131; The claim by 1919 case study patient by Arrah Evart's that blacks/Africans are a result of pederasty sexual encounter is an inherent, Lochner-like imagination, westerners had and still have about Africans. Also see Lively, Masks, blackness, race and the imagination, pp.1-3. Chesterton writes in *Heretics* that 'shock imagination' was obtained in the 12th century in Europe by imaging "dog-headed men in Africa." P.174
10. Regan, p.2
11. Steger, p.61
12. Steger, p. 61
13. Manji, *The Trouble with Islam*, p.6. This kind of I-feel-superior-to-you-but-I-will-disguise-it-in-my-liberal-anecdotal-air attitude is inherent in the self-righteousness of William Henry III in this book *In Defense of Elitism*, pp.10-11. He argues that by being nakedly honest, he'd be taken for a die-hard red-neck or racist, however, he wrote that he's won awards from minority groups (Jews, Colored Americans, Gays and Lesbians) because of his Civil Rights reporting. So he was liberal-minded and whatever he wrote should not hurt because it is the truth, or he's one their side. While this seems to fend off assumptions about one's racial biases, it betrays the content of the inner person.
14. Manji, *The Trouble with Islam*, p.6
15. Kant, *Perpetual Peace and other essays*, p.111; Also see Streissguth, p.76

16. Singer, p.111
17. See Singer, *Practical Ethics*, p. 115; De Waal, *Primates and Philosophers*, pp.140-158
18. CBS Los Angeles News, *Orange County Republican Party Member Circulates Racist Email Targeted At President Obama*, April 15, 2011 <http://losangeles.cbslocal.com/2011/04/15/orange-county-republican-party-member-circulates-racist-e-mail-targeted-at-president-obama/>

BIBILIOGRAPHY

— <http://www.sahistory.org.za/pages/people/special%20projects/biko_steve/archive.htm >

— Abizedah, Arash, *Ethnicity, Race, and a Possible Humanity*, World Order, Fall 2001 http://profs-polisci.mcgill.ca/abizadeh/PDFs/ethnicity.pdf

— Ackrill, J.L., *A new Aristotle Reader*, Princeton: UP, 1989

— Algambi, K. M, *The use of topical bleaching agents among women: a cross-sectional study of knowledge, attitude and practices*, Journal of the European Academy of Dermatology and Venereology, 2010, 24, 1214–1219

— Allen, Theodore A., *The Invention of White Race, the origin of racial oppression in Anglo-America*, New York, Verso, 1997.

— *Analysis of Skin Color Bleaching Syndrome, Somatic Norm Image and Women of Color*, European Journal of Social Sciences – Volume 17, Number 2 (2010)

— Andrew Malcom, *Barack Obama tackles race in Philadelphia speech*, Los Angeles Times, March 18, 2008. < http://latimesblogs.latimes.com/washington/2008/03/obamaspeechtues.html>

— Appiah, Kwame Anthony, *My Father's House: Africa in the Philosophy of Culture*, New York: Oxford University Press, 1992

— Baepler, Paul, *White Slaves, African Masters: An Anthology of American Barbary Captivity Narratives*, Chicago: University Press, 1999.

— Bandes, Susan A., *The passion of law*, New York: University Press, 1999

— Bederman, Gail, *Manliness and Civilization: a cultural history of gender and race in the in the United States, 1880-1917*, Chicago: UP, 1996

— Bigham, Darrel E. *On Jordan's Banks: Emancipation and Its Aftermath in the Ohio River Valley*, Lexington, Kentucky University Press, pp.86-91, 2006.

— Biko, Stephen Bantu, *quotations in South African History Online*, Newspaper clipping : City Press, Sunday 9 September 2007

— Biko, Steve and Stubbs, Aelred, *I like what I write: selected writings*, Chicago: University Press, 2002

— Briley, John, *Cry Freedom*, Oxford: University Press, 2000.

—Cashmore, Ernest & Jennings, James, *Racism: Essential Readings*, London: SAGE Publication, 2001.

—Charles, Christopher A. D., *Skin Bleachers' Representations of Skin Color in Jamaica*, Journal of Black Studies Volume 40 Number 2 November 2009 153-170

—Chersterton, G. K, *Heretics*, Charlotte: St. Benedict Press, 2006

—Christophe Konkobo, *Dark Continent, Dark Stage Body Performance in Colonial*, Theatre and Cinema, Journal of Black Studies Volume 40 Number 6 July 2010 1094-1106

—Conrad, Joseph, *The Nigger of the Narcissus*, Sydney: Accessible Publishing System, 2008.

—Craven, Hamilton, *What's New in Science and Race since the 1930?: Anthropologists and Racial Essentialism*, Historian, Volume 72, Issue 2, pages 299–320, Summer 2010

—Crummell, Alexander, and J.R Oldfield, *Civilization and Black progress: selected writings of Alexander Crummell on the south*, Charlottesville: University of Virginia Press, 1995

—Davis, Robert C., *Christian Slaves, Muslim Masters: White Slavery in the Mediterranean*, the Barbary coast and Italy, 1500 – 1800, New York; Palgrave MacMillan, 2003.

—Dawkins, Richard, *The God Delusion*, New York: Marine Books, 2008.

—Dawkins, Richard, *River Out of Eden: Darwinian View of Life*, New York: Basic Books, 1995

—De Waal, Frans, *Primates and Philosophers*, Princeton: UP, 2006.

—Diop, Cheikh Anta, *African Origin of Civilization; myth of reality*, Chicago: Lawrence Hill Books, 1974

—Du Bois W. E.B, *Dusk of Dawn: An Essay Toward an Autobiography of a Race Concept*, New Jersey, Transaction Publisher, 2009.

—Easton, Hosea, *Treatise on the Intellectual Character and Civil and Political Condition of the Colored people of the United States: and the Prejudice Exercised Towards Them*, Boston: Isaac Knapp, 1837

—Ewans, Marti (Sir), *European Atrocity, African Catastrophe: Leopold II, the Congo Free State and its Aftermath*, London: RoutledgeCurzon, 2002

—Fanon, Franz, *Black Skin, White Mask*, New York: Grove Press, 1967

—Farrakhan, Louis, *The Origin of Blackness*, Final Call News Vol. 20, No 36 (June 19, 2001) http://www.finalcall.com/artman/publish/article_6075.shtml

—Frankfurt, Harry, *On Bullshit*, Princeton: Princeton University Press, 2005

—Fredrickson, George M., *Racism; a short history*, New Jersey: Princeton University Press, 2002.

—Freedman, Russell, *Eleanor Roosevelt: A Life of Discovery*, New York: Clarion Books, 1993.

—Gabe, Khan, *Breivik's Defense: Danish Immigration Law? April 20, 2012* <http://www.israelnationalnews.com/News/News.aspx/154961#.UEaoro2P1X0>

—Garang, Kuir ë, *Myths and Incapacities; glorification of human weakness*

—Gilman, Sander L., *Difference and Pathology, stereotype of sexuality, race and madness*, Ithaca: Cornell University Press, 1985

—Hall, *The Bleaching Syndrome in the Context of Somatic Norm Image Among Women of Color: A Qualitative*

—Harris, Sam, *The End of Faith: Religion, Terror and the Future of Reason*, New York: W.W. Norton and Company, Inc.2005

—Henry III, William A, *In defense of Elitism*, New York: Anchor Books, 1994

—Hochschild, Adam, *King Leopold's Ghost: A Story of Greed, Terror, and Heroism in Colonial Africa*, New York: Houghton Mifflin Company, 1998.

—Hocutt, Max, *Race: Review of Reality of Human Differences*, Mar 17th 2004 (Volume 8, Issue 12) <http://metapsychology.mentalhelp.net/poc/view_doc.php?type=book&id=2085>

—Horne, Gerald, *The Deepest South: The United States, Brazil, and the African Slave Trade*, New York, University Press, 2007.

—Horvitz, Leslie & Catherwood, Christopher, *Encyclopedia of War Crimes and Genocide*, New York, Facts On File. Inc., 2006.

—James, G.M George, *Stolen Legacy*, New York: Classic House Books, 2009

—Johnson, Joel, *Agonizing last words of programmer Bill Zeller*, January 2011<http://gizmodo.com/5726667/the-agonizing-last-words-of-bill-zeller>

—Judd, Alan, *In game of life, Vick blitzed by trouble*, The Atlanta Journal-Constitution, July 27, 2007
http://www.ajc.com/sports/content/sports/falcons/stories/2007/07/21/0722vickbio.html

—Kant, Emanuel, *Basic Writings of Kant* (edited by Allen W. Wood), New York: Modern Library (Random House), 2001

—Kant, Emanuel, *Perpetual Peace and other essay*, Indianapolis: Hackett Publishing Company, 1983

—Kant, Immanuel, *Basic Writings of Kant*, New York: Modern Library, 2001

—Karl Marx, *Critique of Hegel's 'philosophy of Right'* (Cambridge UP: London, 1970)

—Keim, Curt, *Mistaking Africa: Curiosities And Inventions Of The American Mind*, boulder: Westview press, 1999.

—Kennedy, Randall, *Nigger: The Strange Career of a Troublesome Word*, New York: Vintage Books, 2003

—Lincoln, *African*, Fourth Debate with Stephen A. Douglas, Charleston, Illinois, September 18, 1858. From collected Works of Abraham Lincoln. http://quod.lib.umich.edu/cgi/t/text/text-idx?c=lincoln;cc=lincoln;view=text;idno=lincoln3;rgn=div1;node=lincoln3%3A20

—Lively, Adam, *Masks: blackness, race, and the imagination*, Oxford: University Press, 1998

—Locke, John, Selection from *Essay Concerning Human Understanding*. In Rosenthal, D.M (ed.) *The Nature of Mind*. New York: Oxford University Press, 1991

—Maimonides, Moses, *The Guide of the Perplex*, London: Trubner & Co., 1885.

—Manji, Irshad, *The trouble with Islam: a wake-up call for honesty and change*, Toronto: Random House, 2003

—Marcus, George E., *The Sentimental Citizen*, University Park: Pennsylvania University Press, 2002.

—Marx, Karl, *The Portable Karl Marx* (edited by Eugene Kamenka), New York: Penguin Books, 1983.

—Matthew W. Hughey, *The (dis)similarities of white racial identities: the conceptual framework of 'hegemonic whiteness'*, Ethnic and Racial Studies, 33: 8, 1289 — 1309,

—— McMurry, Linda O., *George Washington Carver: Scientist and Symbol*, New York: Oxford University Press, 1981

—— Miele, Frank & Vincent Sarich, *Race: the reality of human difference*, Boulder: Westview press, 2004

—— *Multiculturalism, Human Rights and Anti-Racism*, Centre for Race and Culture, November, 2010. Coast Plaza Hotel Calgary, Alberta.

—— Nojeim, Michael J., *Gandhi and King: The power of nonviolent resistance*, p.73-74, Westport: Praeger Publishers, 2004

—— Pasley BN, David SV, Mesgarani N, Flinker A, Shamma SA, et al. 2012 *Reconstructing Speech from Human Auditory Cortex*. PLoS Biol 10(1): e1001251. doi:10.1371/journal.pbio.1001251

—— Prunier, Gerard, *Africa's World War: Congo, The Rwandan genocide and the making of a Continental Catastrophe*, Oxford: University Press, 2010

—— *Race: Are We So Different? Understanding Race*, American Anthropological Association (AAA). July 8, 2009.

—— Regan, Tom, *The Case for Animal rights*, Los Angeles: University of California Press, 2004.

—— Sartre, Jean-Paul, "*What is Literature?*" *and other essay*, Boston: Harvard University Press, 1988

—— Sartre, Jean-Paul, *Anti-Semite and Jew*, New York: Grove Press, 1990

—— Schaap, Jeremy, *Triumph: the untold story of Jesse Owens and Hitler's Olympics*, New York: Houghton Mifflin Company, 2007

—— Seale, William (1986). *The President's House, A History*. Volume 1. White House Historical Association. pp. 1, 23.

—— Singer, Peter, *Practical Ethics*, Cambridge: UP, 2010

—— Skidmore, Thomas E., *Black into White: race and nationality in Brazilian thought*, Durham: Duke University Press, 1998

—— Steger, Manfred B., *Gandhi's Dilemma: nonviolent principles and nationalist power*, New York; St. Martin Press, 2000

—— Streissguth, Thomas (ed.), *Slavery*, San Diego: Greenhaven Press. Inc., 2001

—— *The Germany Way and More, Jesse Owens and the 1936 Berlin Olympics*, <http://www.german-way.com/famous-jesse-owens.html>

—— *The Story of Race: A History*, American Anthropological Association (AAA), July 8, 2009. <>

—*Under Standing Race, civil War, Reconstruction and Jim Crow*
http://www.understandingrace.org/history/gov/civilwar_recon_jimcrow.html

—W. E. Burghardt Du Bois, *Strivings of the Negro People*, Atlantic Monthly 80 (1897): 194-198.
<http://race.eserver.org/strivings.htmlhttp://ethics.sandiego.edu/Applied/Race/index.asp >

—Wade, Peter, *Blackness and race mixture: dynamics of racial identity in Columbia*, Maryland: John Hopkins University Press, 1993.

—Washington, Booker T.,*The Story of the Negro: The Rise of the Race from Slavery*, Philadelphia: University of Pennsylvania Press, 2005.

—William, Matt, *Wisconsin Sikh temple shooting: six killed in act of 'domestic terrorism'*, Sunday, August 5, 2012
<http://www.guardian.co.uk/world/2012/aug/05/wisconsin-sikh-temple-domestic-terrorism>

—Wright, Richard, *The Ethics Of Living Jim Crow: An Autobiographical Sketch,* New York: Vicking Press, 1937

INDEX

'N' word, xi, 58, 91 ,93, 94, 95, 96
Afghanistan, viii
Africa, 1, 5, 7, 18, 22, 25, 26, 27, 105, 106, 110
African (s), ix, xi, 1, 11, 16, 21, 22, 25, 29-32, 35-37, 49
African-Americanism, 10
Africanness, 11, 16, 22, 26, 27, 32, 34, 41, 42, 51, 110, 111, 116
American, 5-16, 20, 21, 32, 43, 53, 55, 57- 60, 66, 67, 64, 94, 95
Animaliness, 11
Apartheid, 12
Asian, 54, 55
Badness, 16, 37, 38, 41, 42, 43, 45, 46, 47, 100
Beauty, 31, 34, 45, 46, 47, 49, 60
Beauty Chart. See Beauty
Being (Existentialist), 5, 57, 79, 80
Berry, Halle, 44
Biko, Steve, 24, 52, 124
Black, xi, 10, 12-14, 20, 24, 25, 26, 34, 35, 37, 39, 41- 47, 49-52, 59, 62, 65, 98
Black, i, 10, 15, 15, 24, 34, 42, 45, 96, 97, 100, 101, 135, 138
Black Consciousness, 43
Blackness, 10, 16, 20, 24, 35, 37, 39-45, 46, 47, 50-55, 98
Bleachists, 41, 42, 47, 56
Brander, 7-9, 13, 14, 16, 18, 19, 21- 27, 30-35, 38-42, 47, 50, 51

Dubois, W.E.B, 6
Bullshit. See Bullshitters
Capacity, 43, 73
Christianity, 31, 33
Civility Line, 48
Color, ix, 6, 10, 18, 21, 27, 30, 35, 37, 39, 40, 42-47, 50, 51, 53-55, 62, 64, 78, 80
Colored Africans. See colored person
Colorless person. See Colorless American
Colorlessness, 13, 16, 25, 58, 60, 87
Dehumanization, 47
Essentialism, 69, 70, 135
Ethiopian, 31
European, xi, 19, 49, 50, 52, 53-56, 69, 70, 80, 105, 111, 134
Europeanness, 56, 57
Exceptionalism, 80
Exceptionalizing, 80
Externalization, 69, See Externalized
Frankfurt, Harry, 1
Franz Boas, 51, 52, See Boas
Franz Fanon, 10, 11
Gandhi, Mahatma, 79, 99, 107
Hitler, Adolf, 13,67
Hominidae, 24
Homo sapiens, 24
Human nature, x, 8, 13, 27, 53, 56
Humanity, ix, xi, 2, 5, 8, 11, 14, 31, 32, 38, 41, 49, 53, 62, 184, 97, 103, 106, 113, 114, 115

Humility, viii, ix, 13, 18, 21, 48, 107, 108
Hurricane Katrina, 13, 14, 16
Immorality, 11, 19, 104
Incapability, 7, 10, 73, See Incapacities
Instrumentalization, 35, 61, 68, 81, 85, 113
Instrumentalized, 18, 80, 93, 96, 114, See Instrumentalization
Internalized, 4, 41, 69, 72, 74, 85, 88, 89, 106, 107
Invincibility, 108
Iraq, viii
Japanese snow monkey, 111
Jews, 20, 79, 80, 111
King, Martin Luther (jr), 64, 107
Lambede, Anthony, 21
Libya, viii
Malcolm X, 107
Manji, Irshad, 106, See The Trouble with Islam
Master (s), 8-12, 26, 60, 87, 93
Mau Mau, 26
Mentally duped colored African, 26
Mentally Muscled Colored African, 23, 24, 26
Mentals, 5, 9, 23
Metaphor, 35
Metaphorization, 46, See Metaphorize
Mid-Thought Pause, 33, 44, 50, 87, 77, 103, 86, 96, 107
Minority, 6, 10, 11, 79
Monkey, 109, 110, 111
Moors, 30, 32, 93
Moral Gauge, 97, 106

NAACP, 94, 95, 196
NATO, viii
Negro (es), iii, 6, 7, 10, 11, 48, 65, 83, 94, 97, 100, 101
Nelson Mandela, 107
Noumenalists, 79
Noumenalization, 79
Noumenon, 72
Objective Circle, 54, 100
Ontic, x, 2, 5, 24, 96, 106
Ontic disgust, 5, See ontic
Oppression, 8, 24, 26, 32, 33, 134
Oprah Winfrey, 44
Otherness, 4
P&P, 47, 62, 82-86, 88, 89, 95, 108, See Power and Priviledge
Panther. See black
Personhood, 9, 13, 35, 39, 72, 88, 89
Phenomenalists, 79
Phenomenalizing, 73
Phenomenalizing, 78
Phenomenon, 6, 35, 37, 68
Pope, 32, 33
Power and Privilege, 55, 57, 62, 81, See P&P
Pulitzer Prize, 12, 16
Raan col piðu, 44
Racism/racism, x, ix, xi, 13, 30, 58, 67, 77, 78, 80, 81, 84-86, 88, 89, 118, 119, 121
Racist, 55, 59, 81, 86, 88, 89, 105, 107,
Self-esteem, 3, 25, 27
Sense of self, ix, x, xi, 2, 4, 6-12, 14-16, 21, 27, 30, 31, 34,

35, 38, 40, 41, 42, 44, 45, 47, 67-69, 71-73, 77-80, 82-84, 87-89, 94, 95, 97, 106
Simian, 18, 19
Slavery, 4, 6, 9, 13, 31, 33, 47, 49, 59, 67, 98
Slave (s), 7, 8, 31, 32, 59, 88, 93, 106, 107
South Sudanese, 41, 110
Soyinka, Wole, 26, 100
Sudanese, 41, 65, 68
Supremacy, 27, 74, 87, See White Supremacist

50, 51, 53, 54, 55, 57, 58, 60,
Toni Morrison, 12
Unmonkey, 109
Unmonkeyness, 110, See Monkeyness
Valuation Line, 99, 100
White, xi, 6, 7, 15, 22, 26, 41, 46, 53- 60, 62, 65, 70, 87, 137
White House, 58, 66, 138
Whiteness, 46, 53-,61, 137
Zeller, Bill, 4, 136

Made in the USA
Charleston, SC
18 March 2013